NORTH COUNTRY ODYSSEY

Coming of age, End-of-Life Family Problems, Brotherhood of the State Police and the Search for a Good Death.

PHYLLIS HALL HAISLIP

WAKEFIELD PRESS

North Country Odyssey
Copyright © 2022 Phyllis Hall Haislip

This is a true story. I have made every effort to accurately capture my memories of the events that occurred. I have changed the names of my uncle's second family, the doctors, my uncle's neighbor and the location of the house. Although I kept a journal during my journey, I make no claim to the accuracy of the dialogue or every single detail. In one instance, I compressed the time to give the story greater coherence.

Charles Hall is pictured on the front cover. The photograph was taken in 1932 at the New York State Fair. Cover design by 100 Covers.

In memory of:

Allen C. Hodge
Charles A. Hall

Books by Phyllis Haislip

The Viscount's Daughter, Book One of the Narbonne Inheritance, Finalist James River Writers' Best Unpublished Novel Contest

The Viscountess, Book Two of the Narbonne Inheritance

The Viscountess and the Templars, Book Three of the Narbonne Inheritance

Lottie's Courage, a Contraband Slave's Story, Winner of the Beacon of Freedom Award

Anybody's Hero, the Battle of Old Men and Young Boys

Divided Loyalties, A Revolutionary War Fifer's Story

Lili's Gift, A Civil War Healer's Story

Between the Lines, A Revolutionary War Slave's Journey to Freedom, winner of the Edith Thompson Award for Juvenile Fiction

The Time Magus, A Time-Travel Adventure

Marching in Time, The Colonial Williamsburg Fife and Drum Corps

Death was only bad when it was degrading, when it caught you sick and alone and lying on sheets soiled with your smell, your fears assembling around you like specters in the darkness.

House of the Rising Sun by James Lee Burke

Chapter 1

Thursday, February 3, 1994

The phone rang, the shrill sound shattering my concentration. Struggling to control my irritation at the interruption, I swiveled from my computer table to my desk and picked up the phone. "Hello. This is Phyllis Haislip."

"This is Jill Howell, your uncle's stepdaughter."

"Well, hello. How many years has it been?" I vaguely recalled meeting her years ago when my Uncle Charlie married her mother, Miriam Thompson.

"It's been a while, but Charlie asked me to call you. He's in the hospital with a heart attack."

A knot of anxiety rose in my stomach. "How is he? When did this happen?"

"He's not doing very well. The rescue squad brought him to the hospital Sunday night."

3

Today was Thursday. "Why haven't I been contacted before now?"

"I think the hospital called your mother."

I closed my eyes, shook my head, and took a moment before answering. "Jill, my mom has dementia. Probably Charlie hasn't changed his next of kin on his records. He called her when your mother died, and she only remembered to tell me six weeks later. I felt bad because I would have gone to the funeral. In fact, Mom's care has been so demanding, I haven't kept up as closely as I should have with Charlie."

"Charlie told me he tried to call you about ten days ago when he wasn't feeling well, and when he didn't get you, he called your mom and talked to her."

Regret overwhelmed me. Probably he had gotten my answering machine, and instead of dealing with the technology, he'd called Mom instead. He had called out for help, and I'd never gotten the message.

"Charlie still doesn't realize how impaired Mom has become. She's quite adept at faking coherence. And even if she did understand, she didn't remember to tell me, even though I see her every day." I took a deep breath. "Tell me more about my uncle."

"I really don't know much. I live in Oneida, an hour away. When I visited Charlie, his doctor wasn't available. That day, we had a lot of blowing snow and the interstate was icy, so I didn't stay long at the hospital."

"I'll see if I can fly to Watertown tomorrow. I'll call the hospital, let my uncle know I'm coming, and find out the name of his doctor. I'll try to reach him or her today. Thank you for calling."

I put down the phone and took another deep breath. My uncle was 87, two years older than Mom. He lived in the small, Upstate New York city of Watertown, about a 45-minute drive from the Canadian border, a long way from my Virginia home. He had a daughter, Charlene, but she was mentally and physically disabled and lived in a nursing home an hour and a half from Watertown. So, it would be up to me fly north for the weekend to see his doctor and find out if there was anything I could do to help.

Was Charlie dying? Several years ago, I trained as a hospice volunteer. I believed that the dying were the lepers of our time, so much was death denied and avoided. I recalled bringing Ensure, a nutrient-packed drink, to my first hospice case, an elderly woman dying at home. She died just as I arrived. As I sat with the woman's son, helping him make arrangements, I realized that the actual moment of death was not as important as the terms and conditions of the final days. Those days ideally should be spent without the loss of dignity, with unfinished business completed, and without pain. If Charlie were dying, perhaps I would be able to do something to ensure he did so under the best possible conditions.

With a sigh, I saved the document on my computer. My writing was already compromised because of Mom's care. Six months ago, she had moved from Maryland to Virginia to be nearer to me. In her time here, she'd been ill almost continually with two hospital stays and a broken arm. Now, I had to deal with my uncle's crisis. Some pundits claim that real writers managed to write despite everything going on in their lives. Yet, it seemed that no matter how I tried to protect my writing time, my efforts were undermined by events, worries, and responsibilities.

I had recently read in a writers' magazine that there were only two stories in literature: a person goes on a journey and a stranger comes to town. And I was going on a journey. But it was not to the Himalayas or Machu Picchu. It was not a Somerset Maugham adventure in the South Seas. My trip was going to be only one of those inescapable family obligations. Hardly the stuff of literature. I closed my computer, called a travel agent, and made the other arrangements for my trip.

I had returned infrequently to the Watertown area, known locally as the North Country. Located between the Black and St. Lawrence Rivers, the North Country consists of small cities, towns, and hamlets, isolated dairy farms, local businesses, and a few, still-viable factories. Since my mother had relocated near me, my visits in the last several years had been obligatory, brief, and in summer.

My last lengthy stay in the North Country was when my father died in 1978, sixteen years ago. The memory still troubled me. I arrived with a strong sense of accomplishment, having battled the male academic establishment in the seventies, earned a Ph.D., and supported myself as a college teacher in a male-dominated field. Still, I found myself crying broken-heartedly at my dad's funeral and asking his forgiveness because I was never good enough. My rational mind told me I had done well, and yet emotionally, I still felt like a child, a child who would never measure up *because I was a girl.* Now, the prospect of returning to Watertown brought misgivings and feelings of self-doubt that were a holdover from my childhood.

Downstairs, I looked out the window at the daffodils in bud in my flower garden, trying to dismiss my somber thoughts. I loved the mild Virginia winters where I'd had daffodils in bloom as early as Valentine's Day. It had been in the news recently that a nor'easter had brought Northern New York and New England to a standstill. The storm had passed, but some places had received 20 inches of snow, added to what already had accumulated. Chill winds from Lake Ontario frequently brought snow that buried Northern New York while other parts of the country were snow-free. One year, returning to college after Christmas in one such blizzard, I ended up spending a harrowing night at a rest stop on the New York State Thruway.

I turned on the Weather Channel. My heart fell. Heavy snow was forecasted for all of Upstate New York in the days ahead. I hated driving in snow and feared getting stranded even more.

Chapter 2

Friday, February 4, 1994

The next day, it was growing light as I drove from my home in Williamsburg to the Richmond Airport. I'd left my husband, Otis, with responsibility for our son Alex, who was 13 and my mom. Alex would present no problems, but Mom's condition was tenuous as she weaved in and out of a sound mind. Yet Otis had encouraged me "to do my duty" as I knew he would. I'd visit Charlie and find out more about what was going on. I'd called his doctor five times yesterday, and the doctor hadn't called back. That didn't bode well for what I'd find in Watertown.

I put Beethoven's Fourth Piano Concerto into the CD player in the hope that the strong strains of piano music would hearten me as I zoomed along Interstate 64. But I couldn't keep my mind off what was ahead. I would arrive in Watertown by ten o'clock, spend Friday and Saturday with

Charlie, and fly back on Sunday. I'd arranged to stay with Agnes, my mom's dear friend, in Carthage, a small town 15 miles from Watertown where I had spent the first ten years of my life. She was 78 years old, lived alone, and was of sound mind. Staying with hospitable Agnes would make the Watertown hospital trip much more pleasant. I smiled to myself. Alex loved playing with words, and he'd appreciate *hospital* and *hospitable* in the same sentence. I wished I'd thought of it before I left.

At the airport, I parked my car in the long-term lot and made my way to the terminal with a small suitcase and a carry-on bag. The carry-on held the plastic over-the-shoe boots I hastily bought yesterday for the trip to snow country. In Virginia, at this time of year, sandals had replaced boots in all the stores, and substantial winter boots were nowhere to be found. I felt like a knight going into battle without armor.

I hadn't flown in so long, I found myself apprehensive as I boarded the plane to Pittsburg, the first leg of my journey. The flight was smooth, but I was glad when we were on the ground. In the airport, I noted the temperature. Zero degrees. I boarded a shuttle from the main terminal to one of its distant branches and walked down a long corridor to a shabby terminal with few concessions. Out the windows, I saw small planes headed for other remote destinations like Erie, Pennsylvania and Portland, Maine.

When I arrived at my gate, to my dismay, there was no waiting area. A few people stood around and others sat in the unupholstered chairs that lined the corridor. Unsettled by the bleak surroundings, I found a seat to wait for my flight. A plane sat on the tarmac, but there was no activity around it. It was so cold I put on my heavy coat. I looked about for a place to get a coffee, but there was nothing nearby. Since it was near departure time, I didn't dare leave the gate.

My unease grew as the departure time came and went. My feet began to feel numb. I got up and walked around. I approached the agent at the desk, an African-American woman with a bright smile, but no information about the delay.

Finally, two pilots, so young they looked like college students, ambled down the corridor, chatted briefly with the agent, and went out to the plane. The agent announced: "Snow in Watertown delayed the inbound flight. The return flight will be boarding momentarily."

I thought back to the heavy snow warnings on the Weather Channel. Surely, I reassured myself, they wouldn't fly if the weather hadn't cleared. Or would they?

With a sinking feeling, I watched as one of the pilots turned a propeller on the two-propeller plane by hand. He was either trying to make sure it was working or evaluating the ice on it. In all my years of flying, I had never seen anyone do this. I began to think I was making a colossal mistake flying north in a small plane in the dead of winter.

When the flight was ready to board, I swallowed my growing apprehension and followed five brave souls out into the freezing weather to the plane. I didn't feel at all brave.

I easily found my seat on what was a nearly empty plane. I got settled, and the pilot announced on the loudspeaker. "Sorry for the delay, but we'll have a tailwind and can make up for lost time on the way. It's snowing in Watertown, but we should make it in before it gets any worse."

I hung on tightly to the armrests as the plane taxied and took off with a roar of engines. The plane bumped through cloud cover, and I only relaxed when the plane steadied. I closed my eyes. I was tired from rising at four, but was too anxious to read, let alone sleep. My old fears of not living up to whatever challenges lay ahead resurfaced.

The plane lurched and seemed to lose altitude. My heart pounded. Being in a small, fragile plane droning along between heaven and earth brought thoughts of mortality. My mortality. I had been brought up to believe in an afterlife, but that was little comfort at most times, let alone at 25,000 feet. I had been at the bedside of a neighbor who was a pillar of her Lutheran church. It had become her whole life, yet as she neared death, she was terribly fearful. I asked repeatedly what she was afraid of and she couldn't tell me. Christian belief in eternal life gave her little or no comfort at the end of her life. I wondered wearily what part those ancient teachings played in my life.

Time passed. I opened my eyes to look at my watch. The flight seemed interminable. I closed my eyes again and concentrated on the groan of the engines.

Turbulence signaled our descent into the Watertown Airport, located in the nearby town of Dexter. The plane, buffeted by wind, passed through clouds of snow. I held my breath as the plane landed with a thud on the snow-clogged runway and slid to a stop. I began to breathe again. I put on my plastic boots, a borrowed hat and scarf, and my heavy coat in preparation to deplane.

"Your luggage will be placed on the runway," the pilot announced. "Do not try to reclaim it if it gets away. We'll retrieve it for you."

I walked out into a swirl of snow and cautiously made my way down the stairs onto the runway. A gust of wind almost blew me over I struggled to stay upright, shocked at my vulnerability. A flight attendant rushed out and took my arm. I thought I'd remembered how bad the winter weather could be in Northern New York in February, but clearly, I had forgotten.

Inside the terminal, I approached the Avis desk to claim my rental car. The sleepy-looking man behind the counter rubbed his eyes and studied the credit card I passed to him. "Haislip," he said. "Are you related to the Haislips who live in Alex Bay?"

"I'm afraid not." His question seemed intrusive, and my reply was unintentionally curt. I would later learn, something I'd forgotten, that such questions were a standard feature of polite conversation in this part of the world. When you met someone, they pondered your name or where you were from and tried to determine if you knew someone they knew. The conversational dance only came to a stop when a connection was made.

The man looked chagrined for a moment, as if my answer wasn't what he wanted to hear. He yawned before giving me back my card.

With the car keys in hand, I again ventured out into the weather. The rental car was covered in 12 inches of snow. A faded green Chevy at least twenty years old, if not older, with rear-wheel drive, it looked more like a tank than a car. I dusted the snow off the door handle, opened the door, and searched inside for a snow-removal brush or scraper. There was none. I returned to the Avis desk to find the agent had already left. I apparently had been the only customer that day.

Outside again, I cleared snow off the back and side windows with my hand. To my consternation, snow covered my coat and penetrated my inadequate boots. Shaking off as much as I could, chilled and disheartened, I got into the car. It had no carpets, and the worn plastic seats were cold as I slid behind the wheel. Taking off my wet gloves, I grasped the frost-covered steering wheel, started the engine, and turned on the windshield wipers.

Wind-driven snow totally obscured the road. I put the car in gear and drove in the direction of Watertown, never exceeding 15 MPH, and hanging on to the steering wheel so tightly that my fingers cramped.

In the whiteout, a car pulled out of a side road ahead of me. I braked, and my car skidded. Muscle memory from learning to drive in the area came into play. I turned into the skid, and the car recovered, but it took moments for me to calm myself.

I crept into the outskirts of Watertown, passing abandoned factories, fast-food restaurants, and factory workers' houses. Dreary buildings surrounded Public Square, the city center. The demolition of buildings had left vacant spaces, like so many missing teeth. Watertown had its heyday around the time of the First World War. Now it looked as exhausted as I felt. The once-proud city claimed one of the earliest F.W.

Woolworth Company stores. The large, multi-storied building, mostly abandoned, now housed a Walgreen's Pharmacy on the ground floor. The dark windows in the towering building increased my sense of foreboding. The sad state of the disintegrating city seemed to mirror my fears for Charlie. He had lived through the heyday of the city and now, like it, he had long ago passed his prime.

I cautiously drove away from Public Square in the direction of the hospital. On the residential streets the snowbanks were so high I passed through what felt like tunnels of snow. Driveways and parking lots were plowed allowing me to glimpse once elegant Victorian houses, now subdivided into apartments and offices. Others were so dilapidated that they looked beyond repair. Faded, peeling paint on one formerly white house had left it gray against the whiteness of the snow. The cityscape reminded me of an abandoned, over-grown cemetery. I took a deep breath. It was important that when I saw Charlie, I wasn't feeling so funereal.

Chapter 3

I thought I knew the location of the hospital, but whether it was the disorienting presence of the hulking snow banks or my anxiety, I couldn't find it. Although I'd never lived in Watertown, I was born in the House of the Good Samaritan, the same hospital where my uncle was now a patient. I had visited the city often growing up because we lived only 15 miles away. Yet somehow, as I navigated the narrow, slippery streets in the lumbering car, I was lost in a small, familiar city, barely worthy of the name *city*.

I stopped at a 7-11 where the parking lot had been plowed and asked for directions. Back in the car, I realized ten minutes later that the directions were wrong. Or, in my frazzled state, I had heard them wrong.

I took a deep breath and pulled into the snow-covered parking lot of a Kinney's Pharmacy, a local chain with its orange and blue sign, and spoke with the pharmacist. His directions took me to the hospital.

It had taken me a tense hour and a half to drive the six miles from the airport to the hospital. The parking lot was nearly empty when I arrived, and I had no difficulty parking. The high-rise, modern hospital with many windows was now the Samaritan Health Center and looked nothing like my vague memories of it.

When I got out of the warm car, tiny needles of snow beat against my face, and the snowpack underfoot was slippery. I struggled to the main hospital entrance. It was closed. An arrow pointed down a flight of icy stairs. A gust of wind struck me as I headed down, and I kept my balance only by hanging on to the railing.

Inside, a blast of dry heat assailed me along with the overpowering chemical smell of cleaning solution. The floor, tracked with many footprints, was muddy and wet, and a pail and mop stood beside the door.

A woman about 50-years old, overweight, with frizzy, red hair came in my direction. She wore a hospital smock decorated with black and white penguins. I saw from her badge that she was a nurse's aide. I stopped her for directions.

"How do I get to room 202?"

"The elevator is at the end of the hall. On the second floor, stop at the nurses' station. They'll point you in the right direction. We're short-staffed today, what with the snow and all."

"Thanks." I forced a smile.

"How did you find the roads? My shift is over at three, and I have to drive to Adams."

"Like a skating rink."

"They've closed all the schools," the aide volunteered. "And they rarely close the school."

"I know. I grew up in the area." I had the impression the woman wanted to chat, but I was anxious to see my uncle. "Thanks again," I said and headed toward the elevator.

I saw by the clock on the wall that it was almost noon. six hours since I left home. Alex would be in school now, and Otis at work. I had arrived, but I'd had no idea that the journey would be so stressful. I felt as if I had been shredded in a paper shredder. I ducked into a lady's room to wash my face and comb my hair, telling myself that everything would be okay now that I was here.

A nurse on the second floor indicated that my uncle's room was down the hall to the right. I found it and peeked inside. It was a double room, but the other bed was empty.

"Charlie, are you awake?"

His facc lit up. "Phyl? Come in. Come in. I'm so glad you're here. Thanks for sending the posies."

Charlie's color was good, and he was alert. He was badly in need of a haircut, and that detail gave me pause. I'd never seen my uncle without his hair neatly cut. During his long years as a New York State Trooper, short hair was mandated, and later in life, when he grayed at the temples, he'd had the gray cut off. To join the State Police in the old days you had to be at least six feet tall. The rigorous police training included shoveling manure in the horse barns and that had built muscles. Even

17

now, under the white hospital blanket, Charlie was still a big man.

I smiled. "You are looking surprisingly well."

"Have a chair. Bring it close."

Taking off my damp coat, I placed it on one of the two chairs in the room. Then I pulled the other chair close to the bedside.

"How was your trip?"

"The roads are bad. An aide told me the schools are closed. But I'm here now. How are you?"

Charlie swallowed before speaking. "I just want to die," he said, and burst into tears. "I want to join Ellen in Brookside Cemetery."

Ellen was my uncle's first wife. My spirits plummeted. My uncle was a strong, easy-going man with a mischievous sense of humor. I'd never seen him cry before. One thing I learned in hospice training was the importance of touch. I took his dry, liver-spotted hand and squeezed it gently.

"I don't have a home anymore," he sobbed.

"What do you mean?"

"I have no place to go."

"What about the house on Washington Street?"

He freed his hand and pulled a tissue from a box on the bedstand. He wiped his faded-blue eyes and blew his nose. "They don't want me there."

"I thought Miriam left you the life use of the house after she died."

"She did. But now I'm in the way. I just want to die."

18

The anxiety that had knotted my stomach since Jill's call rose to my throat. I shook my head. I knew my uncle was ill, but Charlie's despair was totally unexpected. I wasn't sure I understood what was going on.

Charlie stifled another sob. "I've asked my neighbor, Ross Moore, to come by this afternoon at two and explain everything to you. Then you'll know it's not my imagination, not the ranting of a sick old man."

Charlie was clearly upset, and his situation was so dire that he had asked a neighbor to explain what was going on. I took two deep breaths and turned my focus to the immediate problem, my uncle's health. "When does the doctor visit?"

"She was in this morning. She seems nice, an Indian woman."

"I called her several times yesterday before I left Williamsburg, but she never returned my calls. What does she have to say about your condition?"

"Not much. I guess she is used to dealing with senile old people who don't know peas from beans with the bag open."

"I'm going to try again to call her and find out what is going on."

"I'd also like you to call the nursing home where Charlene stays and tell the nurses that I've been sick and unable to visit for a while."

"I'll be glad to."

"I'll rest a bit." He closed his eyes as if crying had exhausted him.

I left his room, my heart in my shoes, I found the visitors' waiting room and called the doctor's office from the phone there.

"Doctor Panbelchi is unavailable," the receptionist said in a voice practiced at putting people off.

"When might she be available? I'm in town only for a long weekend, and I need to speak to her."

"She's with a patient."

After dealing with the many doctors treating my mom, I persisted. This doctor had not answered my calls yesterday. "I'll call back, and if she doesn't speak with me, I'll come to the office and wait there until she does."

"I'll give her your message."

I hung up, called the nursing home in Ogdensburg, and then returned to Charlie's room where I found him sleeping. I retreated to the elevator and pushed the button that said cafeteria. I needed a cup of coffee, and I hadn't eaten since before leaving home.

In the cafeteria, I only sipped the old-smelling, strong coffee and ate a saltine cracker that came with the hot soup I ordered. I'd naively thought that once I visited my uncle, my duty to him would be done. Instead, it seemed like his condition was more perilous than I had realized. I didn't know what I'd been expecting, but I'd never expected Charlie to be so diminished, so pitiful. Seeing him cry shook the foundations of the world, as I had always known it. It was as shocking as if the portrait of George Washington in the hallway at my former elementary school began to leak tears. I hadn't anticipated that

Charlie would be in such a state, and I didn't know what I could do about it during my brief visit.

Chapter 4

At two, I was in my uncle's room when a fit-looking, white-haired man with a bandaged ankle hobbled in. I wondered what could be so bad or complicated that Charlie couldn't explain it to me himself. He opened his eyes. "Thanks for coming, Ross. Have a seat. This is my niece, Phyllis."

I stood. "Hi, what happened to you?"

"I was out using my snowblower and slipped. Sprained my ankle."

"He was cleaning my sidewalk with his snowblower when he fell. If the sidewalk isn't cleared, I'll be fined," Charlie chimed in.

"Thanks for coming out on a nasty day like today," I said. "It's dangerous out there."

"I've been friends with your uncle since he married Miriam and moved in with her. It's the least I can do."

"Ross has been a great neighbor," Charlie offered.

"Charlie wanted me to clue you in," Ross said.

I settled again in my chair. "So, what's going on?"

Ross's brow furrowed. "Toward the end of her life, Miriam had Alzheimer's or dementia. Her son Wally took her to a lawyer and made himself sole heir to the family home, the antiques, and the property she owned. I guess the lawyer intervened to give Charlie life residency in her house."

"Miriam has other children. Her daughter called me."

"Wally cut them all out of the will. And even though the house isn't his until Charlie dies, Wally is there all the time. He even had appraisers in to evaluate the antiques."

I glanced at Charlie, who shook his head sorrowfully.

"What does this Wally do that he can be at the house all the time?"

"He doesn't work," Ross said. "As long as his mother was alive, she gave him her Social Security checks. And after she died, he sold off the lots she owned in the city and used the money to buy a boat and an all-terrain vehicle. Now he has run out of money."

"And he's eager to get his hands on the house and the antiques," Charlie added.

Ross shifted to a more comfortable position in his chair. "There's more. Miriam's granddaughter, Verna, came to town to testify at the trial of her sister's murderer."

Is she Wally's daughter?" I asked.

"No." A shadow of a smile passed over Ross's face, as if the possibility of Wally having a family was ridiculous. "Her mother, Mabel Landis, is one of Miriam's daughters. Mabel lives here in town. Verna asked Charlie if she and her two-year-old son could stay at his house for a week while the trial was going on. The trial was delayed because of the weather, and one week turned into two. And when the trial was over, Verna and her son stayed on."

"I thought Miriam would want me to give her granddaughter a temporary place to stay, but I never thought she'd stay for so long," Charlie said.

I wanted to make sure I had heard Ross correctly. "Her sister was murdered?" I shook my head. "I wonder if Miriam knew about the murder of one of her granddaughters when she was still in sound mind."

Charlie screwed up his mouth. "Toward the end of her life, it's hard to know how much she understood."

"Miriam grew up poor, "Ross explained. "She apparently didn't have a thing, except her looks, when she left the farm to work at the telephone office in the city. She told my wife she had only two dresses and washed one out each night. She met and married her first husband, an up-and-coming lawyer who eventually became a judge. Even after he died, no one was allowed to forget she had been married to a judge."

"Verna acts as if the house is hers since it belonged to her grandmother," Charlie grumbled. "When she'd eaten everything that I kept in reserve, she asked for grocery money. Food for the boy, of course. How could I refuse? And she keeps the house warm for the child, too. My heating bill last month was $665, more than I can afford. After 41 years as a State Trooper, my pension is only about $9000 a year."

"She calls all over on Charlie's dime," Ross added.

I knew from Charlie's calls to me that he still believed in the utility and thriftiness of three-minute phone conversations. That was one reason it was hard to keep up with what was going on with him. Even when I called him, he didn't want to talk for more than a couple of minutes.

"She has parties all the time at the house and even orders pay-for-view movies from my cable company," Charlie said.

"And since he's been in the hospital, there have been lights on all over the house," Ross said. "Verna and Wally are vultures circling ever closer to an ill old man."

"It's a lot to take in." My head was spinning. "Charlie, I see now why you no longer feel like you have a home."

Ross bent down to rub his ankle, and I sensed that he had told me what he had come to say. "I'm sorry about your injury."

"I've been on medical leave for the last few days. I return to work Monday. My wife insisted that I use my crutches today because of all the ice. But my ankle is pretty much healed."

"What do you do?"

"I'm a drug rep. I have a large area and do a lot of traveling."

"I haven't done a lot of traveling in the North Country, but Watertown seems more rundown than I remembered. Wasn't the expansion of the military base at Fort Drum supposed to bring prosperity to the area?" I asked.

"The wealth it's brought is of a hard-scrabble kind: fast-food restaurants, beer joints, self-storage areas, tattoo parlors, that type of thing. It's done little or nothing for the city." Ross threw up his hands in a hopeless gesture, then asked, "What do you plan to do while you're in town?"

"I called Charlie's doctor today. And since I haven't reached her, I'm going by her office and wait until she's through for the day. I must speak to her before I fly back on Sunday. And since the weekend is coming, I should catch her today."

Where's the doctor's office?" Ross asked.

"On State Street."

"That should be easy to find." Ross gave me directions, and I thanked him.

Ross rose without difficulty and picked up his crutches. "I'm glad to have met you and to be able to help Charlie explain what is going on."

"Thanks for coming by," Charlie said.

I put on my hat and coat to leave, trying to come to terms with what I just heard. I'd had no idea Charlie was in such a dire situation. I'd stayed in touch with him, but had no clue that he was being taken advantage of and feeling unwanted. It was not uncommon for greedy relatives to hover about an old person any more than it was uncommon for someone my age to be in the sandwich generation with responsibilities for children and seniors. Yet, that didn't make dealing with the problems that arose any easier.

I was about to leave when two visitors arrived. One was a woman I guessed was Charlie's unwanted houseguest. Having to face Verna came as a blow as if I had run the gauntlet only to be faced with yet another assailant. My stomach clenched, and I swallowed hard.

"This is my niece, Phyllis, from Virginia," Charlie said.

The woman shifted from one foot to the other. "Verna Loatwell."

Verna's dyed blond hair was pulled back tightly in a ponytail. The ponytail, her trim figure, and high-heeled boots, worn down at the heels, made her look young, but there were deep lines on her forehead and around her eyes. Something about her appearance was unsettling. Perhaps it was the shifty look in her hazel eyes, emphasized by too much mascara. I couldn't put my finger on what it was. Maybe I was just reacting to Ross's information.

Verna indicated the man who was with her. "And this is my stepfather, Bill Landis." He appeared to be about 60 years old with a ruddy face and black hair sprinkled with gray. He wore workman's pants, a red-plaid hunting jacket, and goulashes, the old-fashioned kind with metal clasps.

I struggled to be polite to Charlie's unwanted houseguest. "I gather you've been enjoying my uncle's hospitality. It's nice for you to visit him in the hospital." *Hospital, hospitality*, I thought again of Alex. He would be arriving home from school about now, home to an empty house.

"Charlie says you're only here for the weekend," Verna said.

Something in Verna's casual comment set off warning signals. My heart began to race, but I spoke calmly. "I'll stay as long as I am needed." As I said the words, I had the sinking feeling that I might not be going home any time soon.

Verna showed no reaction, her made-up face a masque.

"Charlie seems to be getting better," her stepfather offered.

"I sure hope so," I said, moving to my uncle's bedside, away from Verna. I looked at my watch, then down at him. "I'm sorry, Charlie, but I have to run. I'm off to meet your doctor. I'm not sure how long that will take. The roads are bad, and I want to get to Carthage before it grows dark. I'll see you again tomorrow."

I nodded at his visitors, left the room, and let out a long breath. It had been a grueling day, and it wasn't over yet. Charlie was very ill and in a mess, and I seemed to be the only person who might be able to do something about it. But what I could or should do wasn't clear.

Chapter 5

I had no trouble finding the doctor's office, a space carved out of a sprawling Victorian house. The waiting room had fancy molding and a stained-glass window, probably indicating it had once been the living room. At 3:20, it was almost full and smelled of steamheat and wet coats. I took off my coat, hung it with the others, and told the receptionist that I was here to see Dr. Panbelchi.

"Find a seat," said with pursed lips. "The doctor has a full schedule."

I gave her a steely, determined look, the kind I'd often seen on Dad's face when it was clear he meant business. I had learned from my mother's care that in order to deal with the medical system, I needed to be proactive. In one instance, my mother was moved from the hospital to the nursing home across from it. She was in pain, but the nursing home was unable to get her medications. I politely threatened to lie down in the middle of the corridor in front of the nurses' station and stay there until they got them. Without delay, the nursing home arranged to get the medicines.

I sat on one of the uncomfortable, thinly-padded chairs, I was so worn down by the journey and Charlie's situation that I couldn't bring myself to thumb through the tattered, waiting-room magazines. Yet I was determined to wait until the doctor was free so that I could better understand Charlie's condition.

AS the stuffy waiting room emptied, my agitation grew. Finally, I was the only one left waiting.

It was 5:15 when Dr. Panbehchi emerged from the inner office. I stood. The doctor was about thirty-five years old, pretty with an aquiline nose and piercing dark eyes. She looked tired, and seemed annoyed to have to deal with me after office hours. Perhaps, I was only projecting on her my exhaustion and annoyance at her failure to return my calls and her inability to spare five minutes to talk with me.

"Hello," she greeted me with a slightly accented voice. "I heard you were waiting to see me. You're concerned about your uncle, Charles Hall."

"Yes. I'm from Virginia and only here for the weekend. I'm hoping you can fill me in on his condition and his prospects."

The doctor consulted her notes. "Mr. Hall has four things wrong with him. He came in with a heart attack, but his heart seems okay now."

"So, the heart attack isn't the only problem?" I had learned from my hospice experience that as the body began to fail, oftentimes people were faced with more than one health problem. But I still was floored to learn Charlie had complications. I must have looked as upset as I felt because the doctor gestured for me to sit on one of the chairs. She pulled up another chair and sat diagonally across from me.

"Mr. Hall contracted pneumonia, but that is responding to antibiotics. He has chronic asthma, and he may have a hiatal hernia. The hiatal hernia is worrisome." Dr. Panbehchi paused. "He has had internal bleeding. But I'm treating him with new medicine, and I'm optimistic that it will work."

"What would cause the hernia to bleed?"

"The stomach becomes raw from rubbing against the edges of the diaphragm hiatus."

"I never knew that he had a hiatal hernia." I remembered from my hospice training that sometimes hiatal hernias mimicked heart attack symptoms.

"To my knowledge, he's never had a heart attack before either."

"Could a heart attack cause hiatal Hernia?"

"No. They are too separate conditions." The doctor looked at her watch."

"Could something he had eaten cause a hiatal hernia?"

"Yes, certain foods have been shown to lead to the problem," she spoke impatiently as if she was anxious to get our discussion over with.

I took a moment to steady my jangled nerves before continuing. "My concern is that Charlie is terribly depressed." I briefly explained that his late wife's heir was pressuring him to leave the house where he had lifetime residency and that he no longer felt he had a home.

"I can't treat Mr. Hall for depression so soon after he's had a heart attack."

I was incredulous. "He doesn't want to live, and that seems to make all the other interventions useless."

"I'm sorry. It's advisable to follow recommended protocols." Dr. Panbehchi stood.

But I wasn't through questioning her yet. "Is a hospice team involved in his care?"

"We have a local organization that serves people who want to die at home, but we don't have a unit in place at the hospital. And until he came to the hospital, Mr. Hall didn't appear to need end-of-life support."

I stood, putting aside the feeling that my questions were unwelcome. "Where do we go from here?"

"Since he seems to be stable now, we can't keep him in the hospital. He will be released in the coming week, and he will need continuing care. If he returns to his home, I'll have the social worker put you in touch with the Jefferson County Hospice, although it's not clear if he's qualified for their help. For a while, he'll need looking after, either at home or in a nursing facility."

Although I realized my uncle might have to return to the Washington Street house, I hoped that he wouldn't have to. "Is there a nursing home available?"

"The best places have waiting lists. I'll see that the social worker drops in to see you before you leave town. In his condition, I suspect he'll be unable to make the arrangements himself." The doctor stifled a yawn and moved closer to the door to the inner office, signaling the end of our conversation.

My head pounding, I thanked her. I couldn't help but feel that she was just another harried doctor who had little time for the multiple problems associated with aging. I remembered one elderly woman I'd helped at the end of life who complained that in the hospital she was treated as if she were nothing. For the first time, she said, she understood how Negroes must feel.

I put on my winter gear and went out into the gathering dusk. Snow swirled about me, and from the slow progress of cars along the streets, I saw that the roads were still treacherous. In the two hours I'd spent in the doctor's office, the ruts in the parking lot had frozen, and I slipped on a patch of ice and almost fell. Inside my car, I put my pounding head down on the cold steering wheel for a moment. I realized I shouldn't try to drive to Carthage. So, I headed to the Holiday Inn, not far off Public Square.

In my room, I called my mother's friend. Agnes picked up the phone after only two rings. She must have been beginning to worry since it was now dark outside.

"Agnes, the roads are terrible, and I'm worn down and don't want to chance driving to Carthage. My rental car's ancient and so massive that I've named it *the tank*." I give a tired laugh. "I'm spending the night at the Holiday Inn."

"How's your uncle?"

"Not doing well. It's a long story. I'll see you tomorrow and fill you in on everything."

"Take care of yourself, Phyl, and get a good rest. I'll see you tomorrow."

I knew I had to eat, but in the motel coffee shop, I only picked a little at a grilled-cheese sandwich and ate a few limp French fries.

Back in my room, I called Otis and Alex. I envisioned them at home, Alex at his Nintendo, and Otis dealing with the supper dishes. I was too tired to fill them in on everything and didn't tell them I was afraid I'd have to stay longer than the weekend.

Later in bed, I couldn't sleep. I had much to ponder. If Verna was with her stepfather today that must mean that her mother, Miriam's daughter, lived in the city. Why wasn't Verna staying with them instead of at the Washington Street house?

I wasn't sure why, but something about the hiatal hernia didn't seem quite right. I recalled a story about an aging former neighbor in Williamsburg whose caregiver, after becoming the beneficiary of his will, supposedly fed him ground glass. Whether it was only a rumor or had it actually happened, I suspected that old people have so many ailments such things would be difficult to prove one way or another. Maybe that man had a hiatal hernia, too.

Charlie was in the way as far as his deceased wife's family was concerned. The severity of his condition could just be the ravages of age. Or was something else going on? Dad, also a State Trooper, reported having intuitions from his long years of police work. The intuitions, based on observations and facts, may not have been enough for him to make a case, but he couldn't discount them. Charlie might be in such despair because he had an intuition that someone was trying to harm him. Whether or not his houseguest or Miriam's son, Wally, who frequently stayed at the house, were doing something to hasten Charlie's death, they had made him unwelcome in his own home. That alone might be enough to cause Charlie to want to die.

I told myself that it had been a long day, and I was overwrought. My writer's imagination was probably working overtime. Or did I share my dad's intuition? Ross had called Verna and Wally *vultures*. In the film *Zorba the Greek*, while the old Frenchwoman with whom Zorba has been having an affair was dying, her neighbors invaded her house and took all her possessions. Vultures. And like in the film, Miriam's relatives weren't even waiting until Charlie died.

I tossed and turned. Finally, I got up and looked out the window for a long time. Tiny flakes of snow still fell and swirled in the cones of light from the cars creeping along the dark street as if they were people walking on ice, afraid they might slip. As much as I thought about what I had learned this day, I came up with no easy answers. But I had made the only decision I could make in the situation. I would stay in Watertown until I got my uncle settled somewhere.

Chapter 6

The glare of the morning sun on bright, white snow was so intense I squinted, wishing I'd brought sunglasses. I'd barely slept last night, but this morning, after two cups of coffee, I felt ready to face the mess Charlie was in. He had been proactive by arranging for Ross to fill me in on his predicament. But I wasn't sure what my uncle wanted me to do. I wasn't sure what I could do.

The parking lot at the hospital was nearly full, and I drove around and around through slushy snow trying to find a place big enough to park *the tank*. Snowbanks infringed on many of the available spaces, leaving only enough room for compact cars. It was often said that life is made up of little things, and being stuck with this big vehicle gave new meaning to the old saw. Finally, a truck pulled out of a space, and I was able to park.

To my relief, the front door to the hospital had reopened, and that meant that after yesterday's storm things were returning to normal. I greeted the receptionist at the desk before making my way to the elevator.

Charlie was sitting up in bed. He shifted a little and grimaced in pain.

I took off my coat and sat in the chair near the bed. "I saw your doctor yesterday, and she said that you would be released from the hospital next week."

His face clouded. "So, they're going to throw me out of here."

"Charlie, these days they don't keep anyone any longer than they have to."

He shook his head. "I can't go back to Washington Street."

"You may have to. The doctor tells me there are waiting lists for the better nursing facilities in town. I'll stay here until we can get you settled somewhere acceptable."

A look of relief passed over Charlie's face. "Thanks, Phyl."

"I'll call Otis and the airlines tonight from Agnes's house." I tried to think of something that might make Charlie less depressed. "Would you like a visit from your pastor?"

A sound, half-laugh, half-cry escaped his lips. "I no longer have a pastor."

"I thought you were a member of the First Baptist Church on Public Square."

"That was Ellen's church, and how she loved that old stone church. She'd been a member her whole life."

"You are no longer a member?"

Charlie shook his head. "When I was about to marry Miriam, I had to sell the house where Ellen and I lived happily for forty years." He smiled sadly before continuing. "She'd inherited the house from her parents, and we never had to pay rent or a mortgage. I didn't want to spend the money from the house on Miriam. It didn't seem right. So, I gave the proceeds from the house to Ellen's church."

"That was very nice." The house had fallen into disrepair after Ellen's death, and Charlie had been so alone that I had been happy when he married Miriam. He had sold the house to Miriam's nephew. Now after what Ross had told me yesterday, I wondered if he had gotten full value for the property.

"No, it wasn't nice." Charlie frowned. "As soon as the church got the money, the whispers started. Where did Charlie Hall get that kind of money? Everyone knew State Troopers didn't make much, and the word went around that I got the money as a payoff from bootleggers during prohibition. Or some people said it was payoff money from gamblers. The tongues of the church members twisted my generosity into a tale of deceit. I still pay my dues to the church. But I've never been back."

"I'm sorry, Charlie. I've never known anyone more honest than you and my dad. How did such stories get started?"

"Before I entered the State Police in 1929, I was a big, strong guy, and I worked as a bouncer and a dealer at an illegal gambling place, back in the woods. But I NEVER took any money, and the stories implied I was a dishonest Trooper."

"I'd stake my life on your honesty."

A young woman with red cheeks and a mass of dark hair knocked on the open, hospital-room door. Lipstick stained her teeth. "Mr. Hall. I'm Janet Doney, the social worker in charge of your discharge."

I introduced myself.

"I'm glad to see you." The social worker took a seat. "Mr. Hall, you will be discharged from the hospital this coming week. You will need either nursing-home care or home care. Since nursing home placement at the moment is problematic, for the time being, we'll plan on sending you home. That will entail a hospital bed and other medical equipment along with around-the-clock nursing care. Before your discharge, I'll keep looking for a nursing-home opening."

"Is there any chance I could go to the Henry Keep Home?" Charlie asked.

"It's the best nursing facility in the area," Ms. Doney said. "And there is a long waiting list for available rooms. You will have to look at other options for long-term placement."

"I'll look into it," I said. "But I'm not clear, Charlie, are you interested in the Henry Keep Home as a temporary or a permanent placement?"

"I no longer have a home." Charlie's eyes clouded.

I turned to the discharge coordinator. "Do you have a list of other senior housing options?"

Ms. Doney took a list from her clipboard and passed it to me. I caught a whiff of the lavender perfume she was wearing.

"Thank you. I'll get on it."

The social worker stood. "Let me know if I can be of help. And I hope you are feeling better soon, Mr. Hall." She exited the room and disappeared.

"Since there is a chance, you might have to have home care, Charlie, the first thing I need to do is to ask your unwanted houseguest to leave."

"You'll have to go by the house to see her. I'm sure she'll be there. And I'd like my bankbooks. They're in a metal box in the bottom drawer of my dresser. You'll find the key to the box taped underneath the same drawer."

"I'll do that this morning, and be back after lunch."

"All this has made me tired. I'll get a nap and see you later." Charlie pushed the control that lowered the head of his bed and closed his eyes.

I left the hospital filled with dread. I was not looking forward to confronting Verna, but it had to be done. What had I gotten myself into? It was hard to believe Wally and Verna were evil people taking advantage of my uncle. They were probably just poor unfortunates trying to get along the best way they could. And I had committed myself to finding a place for Charlie to stay. With a sinking feeling, I wondered how I'd accomplish that daunting task.

Chapter 7

I drove to the house on Washington Street and parked in front. Snow covered the roof and icicles like giant stalactites hung from the eves and disappeared into the waist-high snow. The house predated the Victorian era, and remnants of peeling white gingerbread on the porch suggested the house had been updated in the 19th century. The gingerbread had been painted so many times it had lost its definition. Green asbestos shingles on the house probably should have been removed years ago. One of the hodgepodge additions to the house sagged, and overall, the house looked as sad and neglected as Charlie did.

The snow in the driveway had only been shoveled the length of a car and a battered, gray Dodge Charger sat in the cleared area. The rest of the driveway was filled with snow, two-to-three feet deep. A big drift almost obscured the garage door. The garage looked like it was once a stable and had barn doors instead of a retractable garage door. The sidewalk and path to the front porch hadn't been shoveled since yesterday's snow.

The temperature was in the single digits this morning, but the late morning sun was beginning to melt the snow, and my boots squished in the slush on the sidewalk and the front steps. I rang the doorbell, my heart thudding. No one answered. Perhaps the doorbell wasn't working. I listened and heard the muffled sound of a TV.

I knocked on the door and waited. No one came. But I no longer heard the TV. I was about to turn and walk away when Verna opened the door. She was wearing flip-flops, gray sweatpants, and a hot-pink, long-sleeved sweatshirt. 'Kiss me" was spelled out in rhinestones on the front of her sweatshirt. She looked at me warily out of bloodshot eyes.

"What do you want?"

"May I come in?"

"It isn't a good time."

"Charlie wants a couple of things from the house."

Verna didn't seem to know what to do. "I guess it will be all right." She held the door open for me to enter. The hallway smelled of stale cigarette smoke. I thought about my uncle's asthma and his recent pneumonia.

A middle-aged man, not as tall as Verna, with pencil-thin lips and sandy-colored hair carefully combed over a bald spot, joined us in the hallway.

"You must be Miriam's son, Wallace," I said pleasantly. "I'm Charlie's niece, Phyllis."

The man didn't look me in the eyes. "Wally," he said brusquely as if I should know better than to address him as Wallace. "I remember you, even if you don't remember me."

I was taken aback. I must have met Wally years before at Miriam's wedding to Charlie. But he was so nondescript, he wasn't the sort of person one would remember. Now I studied him for a moment. By getting his mother to change her will, he had outfoxed his siblings. He was a man to be reckoned with. "I'm sorry. Your mother's wedding was a long time ago, and I met a lot of new people on a very short visit."

Wally gave me an exasperated look. "If you really must get something, I'll show you to Charlie's room."

I was uneasy as I slipped off my boots on the rug beside the front door, took off my coat, and hung it on the coat rack in the hall. It only occurred to me later that no one had invited me to take off my coat. It was clear, however, from the moment of my arrival that I was unwelcome.

I followed Wally past an oriental vase on a small stand that stood under a framed map of the Saint Lawrence River. He led the way to the stairs at the end of the hall, and Verna trailed behind us. The stairs were narrow and steep, difficult for an old man in poor health to navigate.

At the top of the stairs, Wally stopped at an open door to a bedroom. "This is Charlie's room." It was in the front of the house, and a window looked out at what I assumed was Ross Moore's house across the street.

"It shouldn't take me long," I said, willing them to leave. But they stood silently in the doorway, like gargoyles guarding a cathedral. I could feel their eyes following my every move as if they thought I was going to steal something.

I surveyed the room, recognizing the maple bedroom set that was in Charlie's former home. Beside the unmade bed was a stand, and beneath it, was an open shelf containing a few magazines and a Bible. Across from the bed was a bureau.

I went to the bureau and opened the bottom drawer. I took out the six-by-12-inch, metal box.

"He's probably forgotten what's in the box," Wally said dismissively. "And what he did with the key."

I had the unsettling feeling that Wally had gone through Charlie's things. He must have tried to find the key to the box and hadn't found it.

I reached under the drawer. My fingers found a piece of Scotch tape covering a key, just where my uncle had said it would be. I pried it loose.

I turned to Wally. "He didn't forget where he left the key." I noticed the slightest flicker in Wally's dark eyes.

Charlie wanted only the bankbooks out of the box, but I decided to take the whole box with me. I walked to the doorway, carrying the box. "Verna," I said to ease the awkward situation. "Charlie mentioned that you have a two-year-old son."

"Alex is asleep." Verna's tone was defensive. She nodded in the direction of a room down the hall where the door was closed.

Hearing the name, Alex, I felt a twinge of sympathy for Verna. "Alex is my son's name too."

Verna didn't respond to my attempt at civility.

Wally and Verna followed me down the stairs and escorted me to the front door. "Can I please see the living room?" I asked.

Wally frowned. "Why?"

I resented Wally's accusatory tone. Yet he had grown up in the house, and probably always thought of it as his house, especially now since he would be inheriting it. With an effort, I adopted a conciliatory tone. "At present, it's unclear where Charlie will go when he leaves the hospital. One possibility is that he may have to come here. That would entail nurses and nurses' aides, a hospital bed, and a portable john. We'll have to set everything up downstairs."

Verna's face noticeably fell. "It's right here." She indicated the door to my left.

Two Easy-Boy lounge chairs and a big console TV crowded fragile-looking Queen Anne chairs and tables. A brass-and-copper bed warmer with a wooden handle hung from the wall near the fireplace. Chinese bowls, tarnished silver candlesticks, and silver-framed photographs covered the tables and mantelpiece. Colorful building blocks and half-a-dozen Hot Wheels cars were scattered on the faded Oriental rug. I imagined Charlie trying to navigate around the antiques and the toys. "The antiques may be in the way."

"I don't think he should come here," Wally said.

I nodded, hating to think of my uncle in the cluttered room. "I agree, but he may have to." I turned to Verna. "He's old and very private. He grew up in a much different time. I remember him becoming embarrassed when a bra ad came on TV. He'd be very uncomfortable using the bedside commode with you in the house. You should find another place to stay."

Verna stuck out her chin defiantly. "I thought he might go to a nursing home."

"I think the best placement eventually would be in an assisted-living facility or in senior housing. And unless he has to come here, I'll have to close this house. He has limited means and can't afford to pay for the care he will need and for the upkeep of this house at the same time." I had not thought all of this out, but what I had said made sense.

Verna's face was set in hard lines. "If he gets better, wouldn't he eventually return here?"

"It's very unlikely," I said. "It's time for you to make other plans. Can you stay with your family?"

Verna's eyes narrowed, but she didn't answer my question.

Verna and Wally wordlessly watched me put on my boots and coat. Even though they may have wanted Charlie out of the house, they probably were expecting him to die. They apparently hadn't anticipated that he'd need continuing care or that I would have to close the house.

"Tell Charlie I'll be by to see him soon," Wally said, almost as if he were guilty of not visiting.

"I'll tell him."

I saw myself out, shut the door behind me, and felt the tension drain out of me like water from a sink when the stopper is removed. I understood more clearly why Charlie didn't feel welcome in his home. I had been as welcome as a visit from the IRS. His information about the metal box and the key's location had been precise. And I had little doubt that

Wally definitely knew about the strongbox and had tried to open it.

When I arrived back at my uncle's hospital room, Ross was sitting in the chair next to Charlie's bed. Charlie appeared to be dozing, but opened his eyes when he heard me approach.

"Hi, Ross, Charlie."

"Charlie said you were due back any time now," Ross said, getting to his feet. "He told me you'd be checking out senior residences in town. I'll be happy to take you to a few places. I dropped my wife off at our son's house, and she's babysitting our grandson this afternoon. So, I've got a couple of hours free."

"That would be great." I gave him a grateful smile. "I'm not very comfortable driving my tank of a rental car on the icy streets, and I don't know my way around. Charlie, here's your strongbox and key. I suspect somebody might have been going through your things."

Charlie shook his head sadly. "I'd like you to keep the cashbox and the key for the time being. I trust you, but not them."

"Sure," I said, sitting for a moment beside him and taking his hand. "I explained to Verna that you'd either be returning to Washington Street with nursing care or going to some other facility. I made it clear that in either case, it was time for her to leave. I could tell she didn't like it very much."

"She must think that once I'm out of the way, she can stay on in the house. That I'll go on paying all the bills."

"I explained that you wouldn't be able to afford the upkeep on the house because you'll need some sort of continuing care," I said. "But I got the feeling she wasn't about to go anywhere."

"Miriam's daughter, Jill, has always been like a daughter to me. Maybe if you call her, she can convince Verna to leave."

"It's worth a try," I said hesitantly, wondering why hadn't this *daughter* hadn't come to his aid? "Do you have her phone number?"

"There's a list of numbers on a pad near the phone in the house."

"I'll look for it the next time I'm there."

"Did you see Wally?" Ross asked. "I saw his vehicle on the street when I left for the hospital."

"Yes," I said. "Charlie, Wally said he's going to come by to see you soon."

Charlie frowned. "He'll come by when he wants something."

"I'll look at a few places on the housing list. Then I'm going to head to Carthage." It was my turn to shake my head sadly. "I have to see if Agnes can keep me a few more days, change my plane reservations, and call home." I let go of his hand and stood. "I'll come by tomorrow morning to give you the rundown on the senior housing options."

Ross drove me first to Midtown Towers, a high-rise, federally subsidized housing project overlooking the Black River, consisting of handicap-accessible apartments. Charlie's income was probably low enough to qualify for residency. The place was fairly new, if somewhat institutional-looking with cement-block construction.

We went into the lobby. A woman wearing a chenille housecoat and slippers, pushing a walker, made her way to a bank of mailboxes. I approached her with a smile. "Hello. We're considering this as a possible place for my uncle to live. How do you like it here?"

The woman's face reddened with embarrassment. "It's very convenient." She turned away. She hadn't bothered to put in her false teeth, if she had some, for her trip to the mailbox.

That wasn't exactly the information I was looking for. I stepped back, allowing the woman to get her mail. She put it into the bike basket attached to her walker and headed in the direction of the elevator without looking at me.

No administrator was available to talk about the apartments or show me one. But it was Saturday, and all I could do was pick up an application from a rack of brochures and tax forms in the foyer. I left the bleak facility hoping that Charlie wouldn't have to move there.

From there, we went to Ballantine Apartments. Here, as we entered the front door the overpowering smell of urine greeted us. Charlie would have to share a room in this old house in need of renovation. I signaled to Ross that the facility wasn't acceptable. We drove from there to the village of Champion, where a series of apartments had been set up in an old motel. I didn't like the look of this place either.

"There's no need for us to get out of the car," I said.

Ross smiled grimly. "I wanted you to see what was available before I made a suggestion."

I looked at him curiously. "I'm open. I can't say I'm enthused about what I've seen."

"Charlie's daughter, Charlene, is in a nursing home in Ogdensburg run by United Helpers. They have a good reputation. United Helpers is a non-profit originally established by the area churches. I believe they have an assisted-living facility there."

"I'm my cousin's guardian, and I have visited her in Ogdensburg. I've been very pleased with her care." I took out the list of places, feeling an uplifting of hope. "Yes, they do have a facility there. It would be great for Charlie to be close to his daughter."

"Does she know him? Charlie never talks about her."

"Sure. She's brain-damaged and crippled, but she has the intelligence of a twelve-year-old. She can read and write, and knows and loves her father."

"It may be worth taking a look at it then," Ross said.

"I agree." I nodded my head thoughtfully. "Although he may need a nursing home for a while, he's been living independently since Miriam died. Assisted living might be the right combination of services and independence for him. I'll give them a call and see if I can visit tomorrow. It's only 70 miles away."

Ross drove me back to the hospital parking lot. I thanked him and prepared to get out of the car. He put out a hand to stop me.

"There's one more thing," he said, hesitating for a moment. "Charlie told me he was vomiting up anything he tried to eat or drink. Could he have inadvertently poisoned himself?" He frowned. "Maybe he drank spoiled milk or something. Or taken the wrong medicine? Old people sometimes get mixed up."

My pulse began to race at the mention of poisoning. "I can't believe Charlie mixed up his medication. He's as sharp as aged New York State cheese."

"I don't recall Charlie ever complaining about stomach problems before."

"I said that to the doctor, and she said he never had a heart attack before either."

Ross raised his eyebrows and shook his head. I thanked him again. Standing in front of *the tank*, I watched Ross's car exit the hospital parking lot. I thought I was just overwrought when I had been suspicious of Wally and Verna. Did Ross, too, suspect them? The next time I saw the doctor, I'd ask her if Charlie could possibly have been poisoned.

Chapter 8

As I drove toward Carthage on State Route 3, the sun was already low in the sky and the road was icy where snowmelt had pooled and then frozen. It seemed like it had been a week or more since I had left home, and today, only my second day, wasn't over yet. I still had to fill in Agnes and my family about Charlie's situation and make plans to extend my stay.

Most of my early life was spent in the area. Now my exhaustion and anxiety heightened my perceptions, stripping away whatever rosy patina remained of the past, and I looked with fresh eyes at things I regularly saw in the first ten years of my life. Unlike prosperous Williamsburg with its charming combination of history and modernity, this area had been a depressed area when I lived here, and little had changed. A mall with a Loblaw's grocery was deserted, except for the run-down grocery store. A McDonalds that was new thirty years ago now looked worn and outdated. The sign in front of what was once an upscale restaurant, Partridge Berry Inn, read "Closed." The "d" on the sign was missing.

I passed a Mobil station where Dad once got his cars greased. I had often gone with him and watched with wonder as the car ascended on a round-cylinder, pressure hoist. It was no longer a gas station, and the Mobil sign with its faded, flying red horse was truly flying now as it hung by one wire in front of the abandoned building.

I came to an ancient dam and power plant on the Black River where colored lights once illuminated the falling water. There were no lights now, and I wondered vaguely if it still produced electrical power. If it was still operative, and it appeared to be, it bore witness to the area's aging infrastructure.

At a hamlet named Great Bend for a bend in the river, I saw the cemetery where a tornado had once leveled tombstones. Even as a child, I understood the irony. Grave stones were supposed to stand forever.

All along the road were houses of various sorts, mostly poor people's homes or trailers with pickup trucks or junky cars in the yard and sometimes a snowmobile. As I passed one trailer with a built-on room, a black-and-brown mongrel barked and chased my car for a distance. Had this area always looked so depressed, so dismal, or was it only my own low spirits that made it appear so?

My mood lifted a little in the hamlet of Herrings, where there was once a State Police substation. With its brown siding and white trim, the substation, now a private residence, looked just the same as had in the early 1950s.

When I was a child, Troopers couldn't live in the same town with their families. They lived in barracks, where like firefighters, they could be called on around the clock. So, Dad lived five miles from Carthage at this substation. He stayed at home only four nights a month. On his nights off, I rode with Mom to pick him up, and it was my job to go into the police station to get him. The Troopers towered above me like tall trees and always had a stick of gum or a piece of candy for me.

A wooded lot still sat along one side of the property. Each May, Dad would take me there to hunt for Mayflowers. I remember how lightly he would hold in his big hand the ones I had picked.

Heartened by the memory, I drove slowly on, winding along the sinuous route that followed the Black River. The road was in good repair, better than I remembered, and the last rays of the setting sun turned the snowbanks to rose gold.

The sun disappeared as I approached Carthage. In the blue twilight, I passed the deserted machine shop where Dad had taken his hand lawnmower to have the blades sharpened. An abandoned factory nearby had been converted into a dry-cleaning plant, but that too had long been closed.

I spotted a derelict silo-like structure along the side of the railroad tracks. I vaguely rmembered going there with my mother for coal.

Carthage had only a few of the imposing Victorian houses like the ones that had once been the pride of Watertown. For the most part, the houses here had been factory workers' homes. Four paper mills, their logs harvested in the nearby

Adirondack Mountains, once operated along this stretch of the river that cut the small town into two.

I passed several brightly painted houses. They stood out against the snow, deeper here than in Watertown. Some sported pink-and-purple, plastic butterflies stuck on the side of the house. Others had shutters with half-moon cutouts. Whether these adornments were a desire to make the world a more beautiful place or an expression of whimsy, in either case, they alleviated the gloom of the departing day.

Agnes's house looked exactly as it had forty years ago, except that its gray siding had recently been renewed and the porch was freshly painted. The house was a block from the abandoned railroad station, where Agnes's husband, now deceased, had worked. I looked in vain for a place to park *the tank*. Amid the six-foot-high snowbanks, the few parking places shoveled or plowed were occupied.

Agnes must have been watching for me. She came out on the porch in her coat and pointed to the driveway of the small garage on the side of the house. Her neatly coiffed hair was dyed blond, and she moved around with the energy and agility of a young girl.

I edged *the tank* into the driveway. The ungainly car hung out into the street about two feet. If a snowplow went by during the night, it could clip the back bumper of the car. I was too tired to care. And there was much I still needed to do.

Agnes ushered me into the warm house that smelled of lemon furniture polish and freshly baked cookies. I felt my shoulders relax a fraction. Her early American furniture had been recovered and her carpets were new, but aside from that, everything else looked pretty much the same. The familiar surroundings were welcoming, and I felt like a castaway alone on an island who had finally seen a ship.

Her eyes sparkled as I gave her a hug. "Phyl, I'm so glad you're finally here. I've been worried about you."

"I'm *glad* to be here, Agnes." I had fond memories of staying overnight at her house as a kid. I invariably woke with a nickel, covered with cloth pinned to my pajamas, and my morning's milk had a jelly bean in the bottom of the glass so I'd be sure to drink all of it. After my concerns of the last hours, how nice it would be to have her look after me.

"Winters in the North Country are long. I'm thrilled to have you, if only for a few days."

"I may be staying longer, if you'll have me."

She smiled. "Of course. You know you're welcome for as long as you need to stay."

I thanked her and filled her in on the trauma of the last two days. I didn't tell her that I suspected that Miriam's relatives might have done something to harm Charlie. I couldn't imagine this good-hearted soul would believe it. I wasn't sure I believed it myself.

Agnes reheated the casserole she had made for last night, and we sat in the cheery kitchen with its yellow-plaid wallpaper. I tried to enjoy the tasty, hot meal, but was too wired to be hungry. I ate what I could and made appreciative noises. After dinner, I called home and explained that I needed to stay longer. Otis assured me they were doing okay and that I should stay as long as necessary.

"Your mom is doing okay," Otis said. "We've seen her every day. She realizes that something is wrong and that's made her agitated."

"Thanks." Otis had often told me that I didn't need to visit my mother every day, and now he and Alex were doing it.

"Alex and I have just had a pizza, and we miss you."

"I miss you too. I'm going to call the airline. I'll plan on returning next weekend."

I chatted for a few minutes with Alex, asking about school and telling him about all the snow in Watertown.

Feeling dispirited, I hung up the phone and called the airline. Because of the weather, there had been many flight cancelations. This simple chore took more than an hour. I arranged to return home the following Saturday. By then, I should have Charlie settled somewhere.

When I finished, Agnes produced a movie she had rented. "I thought you might need a diversion, a chance to unwind."

"How thoughtful."

We settled on the couch to watch the movie. I put my feet up on the sturdy, green hassock, relieved to be spared more conversation.

Having made plans to extend my stay didn't ease my anxiety. Later that night, in the pink upstairs bedroom that once belonged to Agnes's daughter, I again tossed and turned in the comfortable bed. I couldn't remember what the movie we watched was about. My thoughts kept returning to Charlie's plight. Dad had once told me that criminals depended on the fact that good people don't think others are capable of committing crimes. I didn't want to think that the mother of a young child might be capable of attempted murder or that Miriam's wily son had harmed Charlie. And yet, whatever they had done had upset Charlie enough that he just wanted to die.

Chapter 9

Saturday, February 6, 1994

It was late the next morning when I arrived at the hospital. I told Charlie about Midtown Towers, and he agreed we should put in an application there. I explained that since the weather today was decent, I planned to drive to Ogdensburg to look at the United Helpers facility.

"I'm not sure I want to leave Watertown," Charlie said. "All my friends are here."

"Do you want to keep the Washington Street house?"

"I don't want to go back there. I can't afford to pay for it and some facility, too. It has become a burden, especially now."

"From what I saw yesterday, and what Ross tells me, you'd be fortunate to get into one of the United Helpers facilities, and you'd be able to see Charlene more often."

"I'd like that. Until winter and old age closed in, I drove up to see her every week."

"What's the best way to get to Ogdensburg?"

As Charlie gave me directions, he leaned forward for a few moments, the former Trooper pleased to be able to help. He recommended not taking the Interstate because of blowing snow. He finished and lay back on his pillow, grimacing in pain from the effort. I felt a bit guilty leaving him. Maybe his death was imminent.

I found my way through the old city to the route Charlie recommended. As I neared Fort Drum, I passed a Wendy's, a Pizza Hut, a Denny's and a big Exxon station with an adjoining convenience store and a fast-food restaurant. A sign in the window of the restaurant read: "Truckers Welcome. Open 24/7."

In minutes, I was away from these businesses that had sprung up to take advantage of the military base and was out in the country, driving north under gray and threatening skies. For someone used to Williamsburg, I found the lack of traffic surprising and a bit unnerving. I passed isolated farms with houses crouched along the highway that connected them to a wider world. I slowed for small villages, filled with ancient buildings from a more prosperous time.

The feeling that I was going back in time was heightened when at one farm a team of black horses was pulling a sledge, something I hadn't seen in years. It was probably an Amish farm. They had taken on the harsh climate and marginal farmland of Saint Lawrence County in the 1970s and turned derelict farms into thriving businesses. A little further on, I slowed for an Amish horse and buggy, thankful for the heater in *the tank*. In jarring contrast, nearby an abandoned truck was suspended precariously on a snow bank. The driver, probably drunk, had skidded because of ice on the road and ended up there.

My route began to parallel the frozen St. Lawrence River. In the old days, people walked across the river in winter to avoid the official border crossings between the United States and Canada. I suspected that still might be the case. Verdi's *Requiem* came on the local PBS radio station, and the pensive, moving music seemed a fitting compliment to the roiling, dark clouds and my melancholy mission.

I arrived in Ogdensburg ready for a cup of coffee. I'd missed lunch, and I drove around looking eagerly for a McDonalds or a coffee shop. The downtown was even more dismal than Watertown's, with dilapidated houses and only a few businesses. I spotted a Holiday Inn, but couldn't find the access road that led to it. Where Watertown probably had nearly 30,000 inhabitants, only about 10,000 people lived in Ogdensburg. Like Watertown, dingy bars sat on almost every corner, and state law mandated that they also serve food. The bars were open, but they didn't look welcoming. I sighed and gave up on the cup of coffee.

The United Helpers assisted-living facility was on the outskirts of town and overlooked the St. Lawrence River. The building was fairly new, and the fieldstones decorating the front entrance alleviated its institutional appearance. I felt a surge of hope. If the inside was as well planned and attractive as the outside, maybe this would be the right place for Charlie.

61

I parked and went inside. To my surprise and delight, I smelled wood smoke instead of disinfectant and urine.

From the hallway, I looked into a spacious room with big windows facing the river. A large fieldstone fireplace unequally divided the room into two parts. On one side of the fireplace was a large sitting room with comfortable-looking furniture and on the other, a small dining room. A fire crackled in the fireplace. In the sitting room, four residents sat at a table playing cards. One gentleman with a small mustache dressed in an argyle sweater had fallen asleep in the chair nearest the fire. Beside him, a woman with a deeply lined face sat knitting. I immediately liked the homey feeling of the place.

A spare woman with her gray hair in a bun emerged from an adjoining office to greet me. "Mrs. Warren," she said. "You must be Mrs. Haislip. You're right on time."

"Thank you for meeting with me today." My immediate impression was that Mrs. Warren was businesslike, efficient.

"I'll take your coat and show you around. The residents all have their own rooms."

Walking down the corridor, we met a tiny woman dressed in her Sunday best, and Mrs. Warren asked if I could see her room.

She agreed and volunteered, "I love it here. I was very lonely living alone."

The room with its single bed, chair, and dresser was small, yet adequate. A door beside a big closet led to a private bathroom and a large window looked out on the river.

"Residents have help with their medications, transportation to doctors, and maid service," Mrs. Warren couldn't keep a note of pride from her voice. "We have exercise sessions every morning, movies, concerts, and parties. There's always something going on. I join the residents for lunch every day, and I can attest to the fact that the food is more than adequate."

Back in Mrs. Warren's office, I outlined my uncle's health problems. Mrs. Warren jotted a few notes on a yellow pad.

"He has to be able to walk to live here. We are assisted living, not a nursing home. If the time comes your uncle needs a nursing home, we have several in our system. Living here would give him a priority for placement in one of them." Mrs. Warren's tone of voice was firm, but pleasant. She was clearly used to dealing with frantic family members seeking placement for a loved one. "And we have a long waiting list."

My heart plummeted, and I shifted uneasily in my chair. "Charlie has been mobile until the last two weeks. And there is no reason to believe he won't be mobile again. In fact, he still drives. Will he be able to have his car here?"

"Yes, we have several residents who drive."

"I'm especially interested in my uncle living here because his daughter, Charlene Hall, is in the nursing home up the road."

Mrs. Warren put her pen down on the pad and steepled her fingers. "We have a special policy that close family members move to the top of the waiting list. Usually, that refers to husbands and wives. I'm not sure if it applies to fathers and daughters. I'll have to check with the board of trustees. In the meantime, I can give you an application."

The hopelessness I had felt with the mention of the long waiting list lifted. I took the application and stood. "This is definitely the place for my uncle. I hope he will be able to move here. He'll have to apply at other facilities, but I'd very much like him to be here."

I must have said the right thing. Mrs. Warren smiled, revealing small white teeth. "We're proud of this place and our whole system of care. Are you familiar with United Helpers?"

"I've visited my cousin in your nursing home."

"We have several facilities."

I took the brochure she handed me. "I'll keep you apprised of my uncle's progress. He'll leave the hospital this coming week, and will probably have to stay at a nursing home until I find him a permanent placement. While I'm here, I'll visit my cousin. I'm not sure what to tell her. I can imagine she's wondered why her father hasn't visited her lately."

"I find the truth always works best," Mrs. Warren said.

"Of course. Still, I won't mention that he might be able to come to Ogdensburg. I don't want to raise her hopes in case there won't be a room here for him."

I thanked Mrs. Warren, retrieved my coat, and walked through the plowed parking area to *the tank*. Black clouds still hung over the river and the biting wind made me pull my unbuttoned coat tightly about me. I drove the short distance to my cousin's nursing home.

Inside, the attractively painted and well-appointed nursing home smelled of pine trees as I remembered from past visits. A toothy young receptionist at the front desk directed me to Charlene's room on the second floor.

Charlene looked up from the word-find puzzle she was doing when I entered. She wore a green-velour pantsuit that set off her bright pink nails, and her thick blond hair had been recently cut and styled.

"Hello, Charlene," I said.

For a moment, she didn't recognize me. Then a smile spread across her face. "Phyllis, what are you doing here?"

A nurse stuck her head in the door.

"I have company," Charlene crowed. "Could you please bring us cups of tea?"

The nurse smiled. "I'd be happy to, Miss Charlene."

Over a most welcome, fragrant cup of mint tea, I explained that her father was in the hospital and that I'd come north to check on him."

"Oh dear, oh dear. Now I understand why my old father hasn't visited for a while."

"You'll be seeing him again soon," I assured her, hoping what I said was true.

I steered the conversation to pleasanter topics until it was time for me to head back to Watertown.

"Come and see me again," Charlene said as I stood to leave.

"You can count on it." I gave her a hug and departed.

Our visit had been pleasant, but I was heavy-hearted as I left the nursing home. Charlene had a series of brain operations between the ages of four and five. Her parents kept her at home as long as they were able. Now in middle age, she had been a resident in nursing homes for 15 years. Life wasn't fair. Not to Charlene or to her parents. And the end of life brought even more complicated problems. Problems I had to deal with both here and at home in Williamsburg. My knees felt weak as I walked to the car. It all seemed too much to handle. How could I cope with what lay ahead?

Chapter 10

Monday, February 7, 1994

The next morning, before leaving Carthage, I learned from the Weather Channel that it was 20 degrees below zero. Where bad winter weather isn't much of a problem in Virginia, here it was a source of constant concern. It always had to be taken into account.

I dreaded the day ahead. I feared *the tank* with its frost-covered windows wouldn't start and gained a new appreciation for the old car when the engine sputtered once and then purred into life. I put on the defroster and waited, shivering, until the windows cleared enough to drive. Only then could I direct heat into the car and onto my cold feet in their plastic boots.

In the frozen Carthage landscape, pillars of smoke rose from the one still operating paper mill and from various chimneys in town. The roads were clear and dry. West

Carthage lay on the other side of the Black River. One straight-line way to reach Watertown was to drive from West Carthage over the ridge on the Tug Hill Plateau. This morning in the clear, icy air I could see Watertown spread out in the distance and snatches of Lake Ontario beyond. The snow-blanketed landscape, the skeletal trees, and the piercing cold seemed a fitting backdrop to Charlie's problems.

At the hospital, Charlie was sitting in the chair beside the bed.

"I'm glad to see you're up," I said, removing my coat and sitting in the room's other chair. "I have a lot to tell you."

"I really like the assisted-living facility in Ogdensburg, and I saw Charlene yesterday. She's doing well and clearly misses your visits. If you're up to it, let's fill out the applications for Midtown Towers and United Helpers."

He sighed and the lines in his face relaxed. "I'm glad you saw Charlene. And if you fill out the applications, I'll sign my John Hancock."

We were working on the applications when an unshaven, white-haired man came to the door. He was wearing insulated workman's coveralls and over-the-ankle work boots, the kind sold for years by L.L. Bean.

"Come on in, Allen," Charlie said. "I'd like you to meet my niece, Phyllis Haislip, my brother Addison's daughter."

"Allen Hodge," the man said, tipping his baseball cap with furred earflaps. "Sixty-five years ago, on February 20th, Charlie and I went to Albany together to take the examination for the New York State Police. So, when he asked the physical therapist to call and tell me he was in the hospital, I came as soon as I could." He held out his hand.

I took it, struck by Mr. Hodge's upright stance and dignity. "Pleased to meet you." I did a rapid calculation in my head. In the old days, young men had to be at least 21 to join the Troopers and that would make my uncle's friend at least 86 years old.

"Your father and I were partners for a time before I quit the Troop," Mr. Hodge said. "In fact, we rode horse patrol together out of Dannemora. During the prison riot of 1929, the prisoners wouldn't allow any of the guards into the prison, but they let the Troopers in. Addison and I drove the trucks out of the prison. We had to crank each one to start it. When we formed the Black Horse Chapter of the former-Troopers association, I was the first president and Addison, the treasurer."

Dad died in 1978, and it had been a long time since I'd heard anyone outside the family talk about him. I felt the urge to press Mr. Hodge for more details. Before I could, the conversation moved on.

"Allen's wife has Alzheimer's," Charlie said.

"I'm so sorry," I said. "My mom is having memory problems, too. Doctors have started her on Tacrine." I took out my notepad and wrote down the name, then tore off the page and handed it to Mr. Hodge. "I'm not sure it's helping my mom, but it won't hurt to mention it to your wife's doctor."

Mr. Hodge put it into his pocket, then turned to address my uncle. "I'm sorry I couldn't get in before. I had a repair job on Saturday, and I had my wife to take care of yesterday."

I looked more closely at Charlie's friend, wondering how could he still be working at his age.

"Phyl, will you tell Allen what's going on?" Charlie asked.

"Of course." It struck me that Charlie was 'calling in the troops to get him out of the mess he was in. Alex would appreciate the wordplay: *troops and Troopers.* I had wondered before if Charlie had wanted me to visit because he knew he was dying, or if it was a call for help. Now that he had contacted an old friend, I was convinced he was seeking help, rather than company in his last hours. That he wasn't going down without a fight heartened me.

I gave Mr. Hodge a brief overview of Charlie's predicament.

He shook his head sadly when I finished. "Is there something I could do to help?"

"I only planned to stay here for the weekend, and now I'll be staying until next Saturday. Would you know someone I could get to plow out Charlie's driveway? It's full of about two to three feet of compacted snow. If I find him some other place to live, he'll need his car. And I'm driving a tank of a rental car with rear-wheel drive. It's costing $54 dollars a day and $.54 a mile. I rather drive Charlie's little Oldsmobile while I'm here."

My uncle's friend nodded. "I'll go by and look at it."

"Thank you, Mr. Hodge."

"Please call me Allen. And if you give me your phone number, I'll let you know what I find out."

I wrote down both Agnes's home number and the number in Charlie's room.

We returned to the applications after Allen left. Then the physical therapist came to work with Charlie, and I searched out the cafeteria. I was dying for a cup of coffee. When I judged that the therapist had finished, I returned to my uncle's room.

"How did you do?" I asked.

"Not too bad for an old guy. I've got strong arms. I broke my arm right arm when I was a lad, and after that, I was stronger in my left than in my right. I won a lot of hand-wrestling contests with this fellow." He brandished his left fist. "But now I'm pretty worn out after my exercises."

"At least, the applications are done."

"Would you help me do my taxes while you are here?"

I admired my uncle's conscientiousness. Even though he was still very sick, he was worried about getting his taxes done. Yet it seemed that once I completed something, there was always some other pressing need. I forced myself to smile. "I'll be glad to."

"All the records are in Ellen's desk. The same one that was in our living room all those years is now in my bedroom."

I didn't look forward to visiting his house again, but doing his taxes would put Charlie's mind at rest. "While you nap, I'll go by the house. We can work on them later on or tomorrow."

I left the hospital in a better mood than when I'd arrived. It was comforting to hear Allen talk about Dad. In the years since he died, my memories of him had grown dimmer. Since I'd become an adult, Charlie had lost two wives and my dad. It was good to know that he still had a friend of many years.

At the Washington Street house, the sidewalk in front was clear. Despite his injury, Ross must have made sure it was taken care of before he went back to work. The sidewalk that led to the steps still hadn't been shoveled, and the uneven surface was frozen solid. I slipped and slid as I made my way to the front door.

I rang the doorbell and waited. The sun was shining, but it was still below zero. I stamped my feet to keep warm. The door finally opened. Wally stood in the doorway with Verna behind him.

"Good morning," I said. "I'm here to get Charlie's tax records."

"Come in out of the cold." Wally's cordial words belied the sour look on his face.

I entered the warm house and slipped off my boots at the door.

"Let me take your coat," he said, not looking at me. I got the feeling that Wally had already taken over the ownership of the house.

There was no sign of Verna's son. Since his grandparents were in town, perhaps he was there. If that was the case, what was Verna doing here?

"I know the way to Charlie's room." I headed in the direction of the stairs.

Wally and Verna again followed me. They stood in the doorway as I searched the desk for the tax records. Being watched made me uncomfortable, but I had no alternative but to do what I'd come to do. Charlie's papers were a mess, and it took me a while to sort through mail, catalogs, and advertisements to find bank statements and tax forms.

I finished and stood. "May I use the bathroom?"

"Help yourself," Verna said. She pointed to a door next to Charlie's room.

I retreated into the bathroom, closed the door, and leaned on it for a few seconds, relieved to leave my two watchdogs in the hallway. Why did those two make me so uneasy? I surveyed the room, unsure what if anything I was looking for. The walls were papered, and the paper with tiny commodes strewn throughout it was peeling in places. Bottles of Miss Clairol shampoo and Yardley Bath Oil rested on a wire shelf in the old-fashioned, claw-foot bathtub. Charlie must have had to share the bathroom with Verna. Like most old houses, there was probably only one bathroom. Probably fifty or more years ago, a metal shower unit had been installed, and it looked awkward beside the bathtub. The two side-by-side made me think of Laurel and Hardy.

My heart pounded as I searched the medicine cabinet for Charlie's medications. Who did I think I was? Nancy Drew? Or private detective V. I. Warshawski from Sara Paretsky's crime novels? I found the usual Band-Aids, Vaseline, and bottles of aspirin and Tylenol. Perhaps he kept his medicines in the kitchen, or perhaps someone had gotten rid of them. I didn't even know what pills he was routinely taking. I remembered he'd taken prednisone for his asthma for many years. If he was still taking it, it wasn't in the medicine cabinet.

Giving up, I flushed the toilet and ran water in the sink before exiting the bathroom. Verna lingered near Charlie's room. Wally had disappeared.

I took a deep breath. "Verna, I'm not sure you understand. Charlie will be released from the hospital on Thursday. He wants you out of the house."

"You don't know that he'll return here." She narrowed her eyes and her tone of voice was argumentative. I imagined she and Wally had discussed the possibilities.

"I've told you that if Charlie doesn't return here, I'll have to close the house."

"You can't do that."

Verna's words were a challenge, and I didn't want to argue with her. I stifled an angry retort. "Please make other plans."

Verna turned from me in a huff, and I followed her down the stairs. I wanted to go to the kitchen to see if Charlie's drugs were there. But Wally stood by the front door, holding my coat, a not very subtle invitation for me to leave.

Ignoring the proffered coat, I went into the living room. "Charlie wants his list of phone numbers."

I found them where he'd said they'd be, on an end table near one of the big chairs. Returning to the hallway, I let Wally help me with my coat. The sullen look on his face made me feel like I was trespassing.

At the hospital in the waiting room, I placed a call to Miriam's daughter, Jill, in Oneida. Maybe she could convince Verna to leave the Washington Street house.

"This is Phyllis Haislip, Charlie Hall's niece. I'd like to speak with Jill."

"This is Jill," the woman said.

I explained what was going on as gently as possible. "Charlie thinks you may be able to talk with Verna."

"I'll try," Jill said. "I'm not sure Verna or Wally will listen to anything I have to say." She sounded exasperated and angry. "I've washed my hands of my niece and my brother."

"Thanks," I said without cynicism. I didn't think anything would come of a call, even if Jill made one. "I'm sure Charlie will appreciate it."

The call helped me understand what I'd suspected. Miriam's respectable family had distanced themselves from Verna and Wally, and in doing so had left Charlie vulnerable.

After telling Charlie about the call, I headed to West Carthage. When I arrived in the village in fading daylight, I drove by the small house where I lived as a child and parked in front. The wide porch, decorated with gingerbread, had been removed, giving the small house a naked, unbalanced appearance. The barn in the back of the lot had been replaced with a garage beside the house. Air-conditioning units protruded from the upstairs window, and I recalled how hot my bedroom had been on summer nights.

Seeing the house brought back memories of the many holiday dinners my family had shared with Charlie's. I had never realized as a child how difficult it must have been for Uncle Charlie and Aunt Ellen on those occasions. I had felt guilty for being normal, and even guiltier because I always dreaded having to entertain my cousin on these occasions. Expiation was at hand.

Shaking off my depressing thoughts, I drove on up the hill toward my elementary school and parked again. It looked just the same as it did 40 years ago. The old part of the building had burned one summer night in 1953, and my family and all our neighbors had watched in amazement as the inferno devoured the old structure. The following day, I watched from the sidewalk as Dad, who at this time was a plain-clothed State Police detective, along with the fire commissioner explored the ruins. They found that the cause of the fire was old wiring. Dad said his work was exacting. He assembled little bits of information here and there to make a case. I had been assembling bits and pieces of information about Charlie's situation. But I didn't have enough information to make a case if indeed there was one to be made. It was as if I kept twisting a kaleidoscope, but the pieces weren't falling into place.

Chapter 11

Tuesday, February 8, 1994

I started the day feeling optimistic. I was making progress with Charlie's placement and settling his affairs. But when I arrived at the hospital, my uncle stirred uneasily in his bed.

"Oh Phyl," he groaned. "I'm so sick. I don't want to live like this." He moved uncomfortably in the bed.

"Where do you hurt?"

He rested a hand lightly on his stomach. "They started me on soft food today, and I've never felt such pain."

I remembered hearing that heart attacks were very painful, and it surprised me that the pain he was experiencing at the moment was much worse.

"I'll talk with your doctor again."

I pressed the buzzer for the nurse and waited. What did seriously ill, old people do without an advocate? I was about to go in search of a nurse when a heavyset nurse came into the room.

"Mr. Hall is in pain," I said. "Can you give him something for it?"

"I'll have to call the doctor," the nurse replied in a harassed tone of voice.

"Please do that. As soon as possible."

The nurse seemed to recover her professional poise. "I'm so sorry, Mr. Hall. I'll do my best."

"Thanks," I said.

The nurse left to make the call.

"See if you can nap. I'll hang around until I see the doctor," I said.

The waiting room was at the end of the hall, and I could see the door to Charlie's room from where I sat. I had a novel with me, but I was unable to read it.

Dr. Panbehchi arrived around twelve-thirty. It must have been her lunch hour. I caught her before she went into Charlie's room.

"My uncle is in a lot of pain. What do you think is causing it?"

The doctor thought for a moment and consulted her clipboard. "It could be gallstones. I'll order a sonogram of his gall bladder and more pain medication."

This was the first I'd heard about the possibility of a gallstone. I suspected the doctor wouldn't have ordered the test if I hadn't been here. I took a breath and asked the question that had been hovering at the back of my mind. "Do you think he could have been poisoned, accidently or on purpose?"

The doctor seemed unfazed by my question. "Poisoning would have other symptoms." Her tone was dismissive as if she didn't have time for over-wrought relatives. "He's an old man. His body is breaking down."

I wanted to pursue the subject. I guessed that different poisons would have different symptoms. If Charlie had been poisoned, someone probably had fiddled with his medications, and that might have different effects than food poisoning. The doctor turned abruptly and went into Charlie's room. She was clearly eager to continue her rounds. I swallowed the bile that rose in my throat. Perhaps I was being overly suspicious, and yet Ross had raised the possibility of poisoning too.

While the doctor was in Charlie's room, I called Allen.

"I'm glad you called," he said. "I've driven by the Washington Street house three times, and there's always a car in the driveway. If you can get the car out of there, I can arrange to have the driveway cleared out."

"I asked my uncle's unwanted guest to leave yesterday, and again today. Let's give her today to do so. I've told her Charlie will be leaving the hospital on Thursday. But he's taken a turn, and he's not doing well. So, I'm not sure they'll let him out."

"What will you do if *that woman* doesn't leave?"

I let out a long breath. "I'm not sure. I'll keep you updated."

Charlie slept away the afternoon. Just before leaving the hospital, I called Mrs. Warren at United Helpers.

"I have good news for you," Mrs. Warren said. "I spoke with the nurses who care for Mr. Hall's daughter in our Ogdensburg nursing home. They reported that until recently your uncle had visited his daughter every Sunday, and what a fine fellow he is, what a good father he has been. I shared this information with members of our board, and they are in agreement with me that your uncle should move to the head of our waiting list. And we have an opening. If Mr. Hall passes the walking test, he can move in next week."

My spirits rose. "That's great news. I'm sure my uncle will be pleased." I didn't tell Mrs. Warren that Charlie wasn't doing well. He had been progressing nicely until today. I hoped this was only a temporary setback. "I'll call and let you know when I can drive him to Ogdensburg for the walking test."

"I take Mondays and Thursdays off, but any other day will do."

"Thanks. I'll be in touch."

I was delighted Charlie had an acceptable place to go. Yet after seeing his condition today, I had a hollow feeling in the pit of my stomach that he might never leave the hospital, let alone go to the assisted-living facility.

Chapter 12

Wednesday, February 9, 1994

The next morning, I hoped to finish Charlie's taxes and to get him up walking. When I arrived at the hospital, I found he had been moved to the third floor. I located his room and went in. To my surprise, he now had a roommate.

"This is the niece I was telling you about from Virginia," Charlie was short of breath and spoke with difficulty. "Phyl, this is Reverend Gideon Salisbury."

"Hello, Reverend Salisbury, I'm Phyllis Haislip." I took off my winter wear and put it on the windowsill. "How are you?" He put down his worn Bible and looked at me over half-glasses. In his late seventies or early eighties, Reverend Salisbury had the lined face of a man of many sorrows. He was surrounded by a circle of light as if he was lit from inside and the light could not help but overflow.

He smiled serenely. "I fell on the ice and broke a few ribs. They hurt like the devil, and they're checking me over. I'm the chaplain at Midtown Towers. I'm not sure how they'll manage without me. I had three funerals last week."

Midtown Towers was one place where we were putting in an application. Perhaps I would get the chance to ask him more about the living conditions there.

Before I could formulate a question, an orderly came into the room. "Mr. Hall," he said. "It's time for your gallbladder test."

"I'll step out for a moment, Charlie, but I'll wait around," I said. "Maybe after your test, we can work on your taxes. And then, perhaps you can practice walking."

"I'd like that."

After the orderly wheeled Charlie from the room, I settled in the chair between the two beds and cleared my throat. "Reverend Salisbury, we are putting in an application for my uncle at Midtown Towers. What can you tell us about living there?"

"Please call me Gideon."

"Only if you agree to call me Phyllis."

"Gladly, Phyllis is a wonderful name. I'm sure you know your name has to do with love, like philosophy. It suits you. I suspect you'll bring your love to Charlie's situation. Gideon was a biblical hero. He did God's will, even if it was against his better judgment."

"I suspect your name suits you too. How do you like living at the Towers?"

"I like it well enough. My wife lived there with me until she got Parkinson's. Now she's at Henry Keep Home." He shook his head regretfully. "My apartment is small but convenient, and I feel I've been called there to bring what comfort I can to the residents. I didn't always preach the Word."

"What denomination are you?" I asked.

"Wesleyan Methodist. It took me a long time to get religion. At age four and a half, my mother died before my eyes. She had a broken blood vessel and bled to death. My father remarried, and my stepmother beat me all the time." There was a far-away look in his eyes as he slowly shook his head. "At age thirteen, I ran away. I was a hobo for 12 years during the Depression, riding the rails. I rode back and forth to California three times."

"You must have had a few adventures." I had the feeling that I wasn't going to learn anything about Midtown Towers. Yet, I found his tale compelling. His words put a human face on the hard life of the Depression Era.

"One time, going out of King City, California, I had to tie myself to the top of a freight car so that if I fell asleep, I wouldn't fall off." Gideon's lined face became animated. "Another time I was forced out of a town near Minneapolis. I had to ride near the water tank on the train, and I got soaking wet. I nearly froze to death before we reached the next town."

"How did you get enough money to keep going?"

"I harvested grain, filled silos, and did whatever work I could find. Sometimes I'd work only for food and a dry place to sleep."

He paused for a moment, and I wondered where all this was going. The hard lines of his face softened into a small smile. "All along the railway, there were people, mostly poor people, who were generous to hobos. And we knew which doors to knock on to get a cold glass of water or a slice of bread. Sometimes we'd get a sandwich or a piece of pie."

A cold glass of water and a slice of bread, the words said much about hard times during the Depression. I loved experiencing history through the eyes of the participants. At one time, a journal published an article based on my oral history interviews. Another time, I tasked students to write about their weekend at the College of William and Mary. Their accounts were so varied and insightful, I contributed them to the college archives. Now, engaged in Gideon's tale, I leaned forward in my chair. "And then...?"

"I joined the army when the military buildup before the Second War began. I was in Pearl Harbor when it was attacked, and I suffered a concussion." Gideon spoke of the attack as if it were an ordinary experience even though he was an eyewitness to that seminal event in our history.

"When I got out of the hospital, I decided to join the Rangers, but they told me I was too old. I was so full of myself that I trained with the young recruits. I was strong from all the farm work I'd done, and I kept up with the recruits and did them one better. There was a little colonel in charge, a fellow with muscles from under his arms to his belt. He saw to it that an exception was made for me, and I got into the Rangers."

"So, you served in the Second War."

"Not something I like talking about."

"I had a neighbor and later a colleague who would never talk about the war.

"That's one way of coping when you've seen the face of evil, the horrors men can do to one another." [The Rangers from Hawaii took part in the daring rescue of the survivors of the Bataan Death March. Whether or not Gideon took part in the famous behind the lines raid, he certainly knew about it].

It struck me as ironic that in recent years, books and film popularized the war when many participants in it still hadn't come to terms with their horrendous experiences.

"After the war, I returned to the Watertown area. It was the nearest I had to a home."

I shifted in my chair, uncrossing and recrossing my legs, I wasn't sure how to bring Gideon back to Midtown Towers, and at the same time I was enjoying the window he opened into the fraught years of the middle of the twentieth century. "I guess humans are a bit like homing pigeons. My mom and other dementia patients always want to go home."

"By this time my stepmother had died, and my father died not long after I returned. I met my wife, married, and set about earning a living. We lived in a tarpaper shack with an add-on, lean-to for sleeping. I was no stranger to work. One winter, I slipped wood with a slip-tongue log skidder to support my family. I gave the woodlot owner $1 for every cord and then sold the wood for $4 a cord. I did the cutting and hauling all by hand. I had a lot of different jobs over the years until I became religious."

"How did that happen?"

It was my wife who helped me see the light. I hadn't been able to come to terms with the war and the terrible things I'd seen. When I learned the belief that man is born sinful, that we are children of wrath and only saved by grace that made a lot of sense to me. After my conversion, I became a preacher in the First Holiness Church."

"I'm not familiar with that church."

"It is one of the offshoots of Methodism. And once I began preaching, it was as if my future took care of itself. A Wesleyan minister heard me preach at a revival. He suggested I should become an ordained minister. When I confessed that I hadn't had any education beyond eighth grade, he told me there was a way for me to study at home for the ministry. He offered to sponsor me. It was as if I was in the Rangers again and an officer commanded me to go on a mission. I felt I didn't have a choice."

"How long did it take you to complete the studies the church set for you?"

"I was fired with the spirit. I already knew the Bible pretty well. I was ordained in 1955, and I've been spreading the *Good News* ever since."

The orderly reappeared with Charlie on the gurney, and I retreated to the hallway while the orderly got him back in bed. I had learned Gideon's life story, but little about Midtown Towers. It didn't matter. Gideon's holiness shone forth like a beacon in the darkness of my distress over Charlie.

Back in the room, I went to my uncle's bedside. "How did it go?'

"It went okay."

"Are you still up for taxes?"

"I'd feel better if they were done." He pushed the button that allowed him to sit more upright. He grimaced as he tried to get comfortable in the bed.

"I figured them out last night after Agnes turned in." I had waited until my hostess went to bed, knowing that Charlie valued his privacy. "All you need to do is look them over and sign them."

He took the tax forms and studied them. I'd been saddened when I worked through them the night before. His interest income had been only $300, not much for a life's savings. "You had a lot more savings interest last year," I said.

"My health insurance didn't pay all of Miriam's hospital expenses or for the time she spent in the nursing home. Her funeral was $5000, and then in October I had to install a new furnace."

"Didn't Miriam have any assets?"

Charlie laughed a bitter laugh. "She didn't have any savings or life insurance. I had to cash in my life insurances to bury her. This house was all she had and some property, and she'd willed those to Wally."

I wondered if the Washington Street house really needed a new furnace or had Wally just wanted it replaced before he inherited it. "I figured that it was the funeral and the upkeep on the house."

"Yes, with that old house, it is one thing after another. Wally wants me to put a new roof on it. He's worried a leak might spoil Miriam's precious antiques." He put the taxes down on the over-the-bed table. "The taxes look fine. Do you have a pen?"

I dug one out of my purse and watched as he struggled to write his name.

"I've already done ours," Gideon volunteered.

"It's always a relief when they're in the mail," I said. "I'll drop these at the post office on my way back to Carthage. Charlie, are you up for a walk?"

"Not now," my uncle said wearily, "I'm ready for a nap."

A half-hour later, Charlie was napping when the phone rang. I answered after the first ring. It was Allen.

"*That woman's* car is still in the driveway," he said.

"Gosh, Allen, what do I do now?"

"I have an idea. Call the house and ask her to move her car so you can get the driveway plowed? Can you meet me there at three?"

"I'll call her and be at the house at three."

I stood and put on my coat. "Gideon, if my uncle wakes and wonders where I've gone, please tell him that I'm seeing about getting his driveway plowed."

"I'll be glad to."

I called Verna from the waiting room.

"Hello," Verna snarled. "What do you want now?"

"Please move your car so that I can get the driveway plowed."

"You need to stop butting in where you're not wanted." Verna hung up.

I put down the phone and closed my eyes for a moment. I was a long way from Virginia, my family, and my writing. I took a deep breath, trying not to be overwhelmed by the difficulties Charlie's situation presented. I hadn't gotten him up to walk, and now I had to deal with Verna.

Chapter 13

At 2:45, I made my way to the Washington Street house with butterflies in my stomach. I suspected that Verna might think that staying in the house implied some sort of ownership. A tow truck, a dump truck, and a front-end loader idled near the driveway. I parked *the tank* and Allen got out of the tow truck.

"Tell *that woman* to move her car or we'll tow it away," he said.

He stayed on the sidewalk, while I went up the front walk and prepared to knock on the door.

Verna opened the door before I could do so. "What do *you* want?" Her words were abrupt, caustic.

I swallowed my desire to respond in kind. Instead, I made an effort to be nice. "Will you please move your car so we can plow the driveway?"

"And if I don't."

"I think it's pretty obvious. We'll tow it away."

Verna studied the waiting truck and the front-end loader for a moment. "I'll get my keys." She slammed the door in my face. With the mention of keys, I realized I didn't have my uncle's car keys.

I stood beside Allen in the cold. Minutes passed, and Verna didn't appear. I turned to him. "Verna has had plenty of time to dress the boy if that what's holding her up." Without a word, we walked in the direction of the tow truck.

Allen signaled the driver. Before the tow truck reached the driveway, Verna stormed out of the front door. She was alone.

I stopped her. "I'll need to find Charlie's car keys. I assume you'll be out of the house by later today. So, I'm calling Wally to meet us here tomorrow morning."

Verna snorted, got in her car, backed out of the driveway, and tromped on the accelerator. The wheels spun on the ice before they caught hold and she drove away.

Allen nodded to the tow truck driver, and he left.

"How much do I owe the owner for coming out today?" I asked.

"He's a friend of mine. As is the guy with the front-end loader. Don't worry about paying either of them."

"I'm not sure I understand. I'm from a world where people charge by the hour or the job."

"It works this way. When they need to borrow my backhoe or my bulldozer, it will be available."

I slowly nodded my head. The barter system was apparently alive and well in the North County. Thankfully. We stood and watched as the front-end loader removed months of solidified snow from the driveway and deposited it into the dump truck. My feet were cold, and I wiggled my toes in my shoes.

"I didn't realize the driveway couldn't just be plowed. Now I see why," I said.

"Yes, the snow's compacted and frozen. You look half frozen yourself. How about a cup of coffee? And then you can drive me back to my house."

"That would be good." I wanted to know more about this man, my uncle's buddy, who had stepped up to help both of us. And I wanted to ask Allen about his time with my dad.

Fifteen minutes later, we sat companionably at a roadside restaurant that had once been a hot-dog stand. Dad had told me that the owner had started out with a pushcart selling popcorn on Public Square and that gradually, over several years, he had made enough money for a hot-dog stand and later on for a restaurant and a motel. Now it was a sports bar with team paraphilia displayed on the walls. Did the man's family still run the business, profiting from one man's hard work and initiative, or like many other American families had they moved on to bigger and better things?

Fragrant, steaming coffees arrived at our table. I savored the delicious brew, a pleasant change from Agnes's instant coffee and the hospital's sludge.

"How is your wife doing?" I asked.

"She disappeared last night while I was sleeping, I found her in the cold cellar dressed only in her nightgown. I've told my daughter Susanne about the medicine your mother is taking. She lives in Rochester and manages things like my wife's medicine." Allen shook his head. "Five days a week I pay a woman to look after my wife. She takes Esther to her home. That leaves me free to work."

My face must have registered my surprise. "What do you do?"

"I've been maintaining the trucks and the other equipment at the paper mill in Deferiet, for fifty years, ever since I left the State Police. I have a crew that works for me. But I handle all the accounts and keep everything going."

"You have your wife nights and on the weekends?"

"My cousin looks after my wife most weekends. And when I told her about you, she remembered your dad fondly. They often played cards together. I don't pay my cousin. But I do buy all her groceries. It works out."

How nice it seemed to hear Allen talk about my father. "What else can you tell me about my dad?"

Allen's eyes crinkled at the corners. "When we were partners, he had been in the Troop a year longer than me. So, he was in charge. And I didn't like it that he was the boss. So, I complained to him. And after that, one day I was in charge, and the next day he was. It worked out fine. He was easygoing and good company."

I smiled. I had never thought of my father as easygoing. "Is there anything else you can tell me?"

Allen seemed lost for a moment in memories. "On long patrols, we would sing. And from time to time, we'd tether our horses out of sight and go into the woods and have a nap. No one ever knew."

"I can't imagine you did much napping in the woods during this kind of weather."

"You're right about that. But we wore heavy sheepskin coats and fur hats and managed to stay warm."

"Did you catch bootleggers?"

Allen laughed. "Your dad and I had one memorable pinch. In those days, the bootleggers came across from Canada heading to New York City. Border security wasn't very tight in those days, and many a car trunk had a load of hooch. We were always on the lookout for expensive cars with well-dressed drivers." Allen took a drink of coffee before continuing. "The driver got out. He was wearing a fancy camel-haired coat, winged-tipped shoes, and had an unlit cigar in his mouth.

'We'd like to see what you have in your trunk,' Addison said, politely.

'Not without a search warrant,' the man protested.

'You know we can get one,' Addison said. 'In fact, we can stay right here in the cold until my partner, Trooper Hodge, rides to Elizabethtown to get one from the judge.'

I laughed. I vaguely remembered Dad telling a version of story.

The following year or so, we got cars and only used horses to control crowds.

The man threw up his arms. 'You fellows got me.' He opened the trunk. It was filled with cases of liquor. 'I don't so much mind getting caught as being caught by men riding horses. I'll never live that down.'"

I took a last drink of coffee, returning my empty coffee cup to its saucer. "Speaking of cars, Charlie's Oldsmobile has been sitting in that cold garage for several months. Do you suppose it will start?"

"Come by my house tomorrow morning at about 9:30. I know a mechanic, and I'll arrange for him to meet us there to start the car. When we get it going, we'll need to take it to get it inspected."

Allen, like Dad, was a great source of practical suggestions. I had forgotten that the car probably hadn't been inspected. I'd gathered that Charlie hadn't used it for three months or more. "I really appreciate your help. I'm ready to dump *the tank* I'm driving. I'm going to arrange to get Charlie's car keys and the house keys. Maybe the car keys are with the house keys."

Back at the hospital, I called the Washington Street house, and when Verna heard my voice, she hung up. I called again, and no one answered. I found Wally's phone number and called him, explaining that I needed Charlie's car keys, and he agreed to be at the house the next morning. With that business taken care of, I walked the length of the corridor with Charlie one time.

"Have you heard any more about being released from the hospital?" I asked when we returned to his room.

"The nurse told me that I had to walk a little better before I could go to a nursing home. I think they don't have a place here for me to go yet."

I wasn't sure Charlie understood the distinction between a nursing home and assisted living, especially since he had to walk to go to both places. "I'm off to Agnes's house. I'll see you tomorrow."

In the car heading to Carthage, I thought over the day's events. Charlie had been able to walk a little today, his driveway was cleared, and I again had made it clear to Verna that I expected her to be out of the house by tomorrow. I'd heard people say that when you were in a crisis and needed someone to help, magically someone appeared. I'd never believed it, until now. As unlikely as it might seem my father's partner of 60 or more years ago was my knight-errant, Gideon, a balm for my flagging spirit, and Agnes, a surrogate mother. How depressing it would be to stay in a hotel these many days. I resolved to treat her to dinner. If not tonight, then soon.

Chapter 14

Thursday, February 10, 1994

It was 28 degrees below zero when I drove to Watertown the next morning. The frigid temperature didn't bode well for getting Charlie's car started. Allen had given me directions to his house on the outskirts of the city, and I found it without difficulty. The white house was of indeterminate age, but from its appearance, had probably once been a farmhouse and the big garage in back had probably once been a barn. I parked in the plowed driveway, not far from a side door.

Allen opened the door immediately. "Good morning. Come on in." He held the door for me, and I stepped into his office.

"It's a bit of a mess," he apologized.

I glanced around. Not a single thing was out of place. "It looks fine to me."

A sturdy oak door leading into the kitchen was open, and rubber bands adorned the doorknob. I had noted rubber bands on the doorknobs at Agnes's house. A North Country custom? Apparently.

"I've just been doing my books." He showed me neat figures all entered by hand in a ledger.

"I'm impressed," I said, and I was. No computer or adding machine was in evidence. He seemingly was running his business the same way he had over the years. I wondered how his employers liked getting handwritten invoices. Maybe they were impressed too.

"We are meeting a mechanic at Charlie's garage at ten. We should head over there now and get his keys." He frowned. "We should have gotten them before."

I nodded in agreement. I didn't trust Wally either.

Allen rode with me to the Washington Street house. When we arrived, the mechanic who had come by yesterday with the tow truck was waiting for us. He got out of the truck, and Allen introduced me to Murph. Murph was a big guy about 50 with a thick neck and red cheeks. He was wearing a padded-down coat and a knitted-maroon tuque.

I went to the front door and knocked. No one answered. I knocked louder. There was no car in the driveway. I tried the door. It was locked.

"Let's try the back door," Allen suggested.

We made our way to the back of the house. A path hadn't been shoveled, and we maneuvered our way by following frozen footprints in the crusty snow.

He tried the door. "Someone has put the chain on it." He mumbled an inaudible curse word.

Allen asked Murph for a wire. Murph had one in his toolbox and returned with it in minutes. Allen removed his heavy gloves, released the chain, and picked the lock. He turned to us with a look of triumph on his face.

"It's been a while since I've broken into a house. I haven't lost my touch. I'll bring a screwdriver next time, and get rid of that blasted chain once and for all."

Inside the house, I found the car keys on a hook in the kitchen where Charlie had told me they'd be, but there were no house keys on the keychain. Wally had removed the house keys. Again, I couldn't shake the feeling that Wally thought he had already taken possession of the property.

Outside again, we went into the glacial garage. One window, heavy with frost, cast a dim light into the interior. Allen found a light switch. The garage was so filled with stuff that there was barely room for the car. Cobwebs and grime covered everything. I found a place to stand out of the way.

Murph got into the copper-colored Oldsmobile and turned it on. Nothing. I was not surprised. The car had been in the garage since before Thanksgiving. The mechanic opened the hood, and he and Allen studied the engine. Murph jiggled a wire, got back in the car, and turned on the ignition. The engine sputtered for a moment and then began to purr. Murph hadn't even had to use jumper cables.

He got out of the car and left the engine running. "I'll meet you at my place. And we'll get this car inspected."

Allen turned to me. "I'll drive your uncle's car in case it quits. You can follow in the Chevy."

Back in *the tank*, I marveled again at Allen for arranging all this. He'd even had the foresight to have me drive him so that he'd be available to drive Charlie's car.

I followed him to a big-vehicle garage near the old fairgrounds. A green sign with white lettering over the door read: Murphy's Garage.

Inside, it smelled of oil and exhaust. Workmen in heavy clothes were working on trucks and a bus. I spotted a nearly nude girlie calendar on the wall. Women's liberation hadn't come yet, apparently. Or had it? Another sign reassured me. "Murph is the boss, ask Mary if you want to know anything."

Thankfully, the Oldsmobile passed. I opened my purse to pay for Murph's help and the inspection.

Allen held up a hand. "It's taken care of."

"Thank you, Allen!" I hadn't seen money change hands and suspected, like with the snow removal, there was a system of *quid pro quo* at work here. Either Allen sent them a lot of business or he was just taking care of it himself. In any case, it was clear that I wasn't to pay.

"Now that you're legal," he said, "you can turn in the rental. I'll follow you there in Charlie's car."

I was happy to turn in *the tank*. The week had cost $356, and I'd gone nowhere except to Ogdensburg and back and forth to the hospital from Agnes's house.

At the rental office, I eased into the sporty Oldsmobile. What a relief to have front-wheel drive. And I was confident it would fit into Agnes's driveway without hanging out into the road.

Allen got in the passenger side. "I'd like to show you the place where my brother, Carlton, is staying temporarily. Maybe Charlie can stay there, too," he said.

"Which way?"

"Take a left at the next corner."

The neat little Oldsmobile took the corner smoothly. *The tank* was like a plow horse and Charlie's car was a thoroughbred.

We traveled through several streets with dirty snow piled in high banks.

"Stop here," he finally said.

I pulled up in front of a gray-stone building. A sign out in front read: Whispering Pines. Named, I assumed for the row of scraggly pines that grew along one side of the building.

"Whispering Pines used to be the old county home. It's now a nursing home," Allen said.

I didn't like the look of the place. And I remembered my grandmother saying in the weeks before she died, "Just send me to the county home." Even as a ten-year-old, I knew that was the same as saying that we didn't love her, and she might as well go to the poor house since the county home was for indigents.

We entered the building, and I was immediately struck by the smell of urine. A man rose from a chair and headed his walker in our direction.

"Phyllis," Allen said. "I'd like you to meet my brother, Carlton."

"I've been waiting for you," Carlton said. With white hair and a slim build, he resembled Allen, but he was smaller, and his eyes were closer together.

With his usual efficiency, Allen had phoned with our approximate arrival time and the information that I was considering the possibility of my uncle staying at Whispering Pines.

"You don't want to bring your uncle here," Carlton said. "No one should come to this place." He moved his walker closer.

I didn't find Carlton threatening, yet I instinctively backed up. "What's wrong with it?" I asked.

"Everything. The food is lousy; the showers are inadequate."

In his eagerness to tell me what he thought of the place, Carlton moved forward again. I wondered if he had to be close and speak loudly to be heard. My back was now at the wall.

"I took a shower this morning, and the water never got more than lukewarm. When I asked about it, the aide told me that was so I wouldn't burn myself."

"Thank you for your candor, Carlton. Normally, I'd ask to see a room. But you've convinced me that this is not the place for my uncle."

"It's an awful place," he grumbled. "Fortunately, I won't be staying here long."

I wondered if Carlton's tirade against the place wasn't aimed at his brother, as if it was Allen's fault that he was at Whispering Pines. From my experience with nursing homes in Williamsburg, I knew that people leaving the hospital had to go to wherever a bed was available. I hoped Charlie wouldn't be sent here.

Allen shook his head sadly. "Don't mind Carlton. He's unhappy about everything all the time. He's had an unhappy life. Yet I can't blame him for not liking this place. I guessed you wouldn't like it either, but thought you should see what is available. We better be getting on. I can imagine you are anxious to see Charlie."

"Yes." I looked at my watch. "He was doing better yesterday, and I had him up walking. I plan to do the same today."

"Don't bring him here," Carlton repeated as we headed out the door.

I drove Allen to his house, said goodbye with a grateful hug, and went on to the hospital. I easily parked the Oldsmobile and made my way to Charlie's room.

He was waiting for me with the walker in front of him. Gideon wasn't there. "Have you been walking?" I asked.

"No, I told the nurses that I'd wait for you."

I pulled up a chair. "First let me give you the news. Your car started this morning, and it was 28 degrees below zero when I left Agnes's house. It's a pleasure to drive after that elephant of a rental."

Charlie beamed. "I'm glad you can use it."

I told him about the inspection and my visit to Whispering Pines. "I didn't stay long enough to talk to anyone or see a room. It's not a very nice place."

"Shall we walk?" Charlie asked.

"Yes. But there's just one more thing. It occurred to me that whoever cuts your hair might come to the hospital and give you a haircut."

Charlie perked up. "I'd like that," he said, a twinkle returning to his eyes. "I feel like one of those dogs that have so much hair you can't see their eyes."

"What's your hairdresser's name? I'll call right away."

Charlie gave me the name of the beauty-barber shop, and I gave them a call and explained my uncle's situation.

"Your hairdresser says she'll come by if she can," I told him when I got back to the room. "Thursday and Friday are her busiest days."

"But I don't have any money."

I took a twenty-dollar bill from my wallet. "Here, stick this somewhere safe."

After walking with Charlie, I left the hospital with a sense of satisfaction. However, as I drove through the gray countryside toward Carthage and thought about the days ahead, I realized that my uncle's future was far from settled. Tomorrow would begin my second week away, and it didn't appear likely that I'd be able to get back to Williamsburg any time soon. Like Odysseus trying to return to Ithaca, I was encountering one difficulty after another. I'd call Otis tonight and the airlines to again reschedule my flights, but first I planned to take Agnes to dinner. I'd take her to the Sahara Inn, a restaurant that had been in operation for fifty years, situated along a lonely stretch of Route 3 about five miles from Carthage. The exotic name had always struck me as out of place in the North Country. Now I thought it should have been named Oasis rather than Sahara. I was looking forward to revisiting the familiar place with its red-plastic booths, dim lighting and hearty Italian food.

When I neared the top of the long hill leading into West Carthage, I noticed dark clouds beginning to march across the sky like an advancing army. We were probably in for more snow. I crossed my fingers, hoping I'd be able to have a relaxing meal with Agnes before it hit. Whether it was the approaching storm or the prospects of extending my stay in the area, I couldn't shake an ominous feeling.

Chapter 15

Friday, February 11, 1994

I awoke in the morning to the sound of the snowplow. Agnes and I had made it out to dinner last evening, and it had been spitting snow on our return to Carthage. During the night, I heard the growl of the plow several times. Now the plow sounded like it might come into my bedroom.

I could see my breath, and dreaded casting off the extra covers that Agnes had given me. I understood why she and Allen – and I assumed other local older people – still wore long underwear. The bed socks that she insisted I needed had come in handy.

Wearing only my light Virginia robe, I went to the window. It was so clogged with ice and snow I couldn't see out.

I hastily dressed in the clean clothes that Agnes had washed for me yesterday, made my way downstairs, and looked out. It had snowed about 12 inches, and a two-foot bank of snow was piled behind the Oldsmobile. I looked thankfully at the car. What if *the tank* had been hanging out of the driveway during the storm?

"Do you need to drive to Watertown today?" Agnes asked.

"It's really important for Charlie to be able to walk if he is going to qualify for the United Helpers facility. We need to practice."

After breakfast, Agnes went out with a broom and I took the shovel. The sky was gray and small hard pellets of snow were still falling. While she swept the snow from the car, I shoveled snow from behind it. Or tried to. Where the plow had passed, it was piled high and heavy.

Agnes finished cleaning off the car. "Isn't the snow beautiful? I love it."

I smiled at her enthusiasm and just kept on shoveling.

On the way to Watertown, I trailed a town truck spewing sand on the road. Only part of the hospital lot had been plowed, but with the smaller car, I was able to find a space.

Charlie was sitting up in bed. His color was good, his hair combed, and he'd had a shave. He smiled as I walked in.

"Charlie, what do you say we do some more walking?"

"Gladly, if it will help get me out of here."

"How are you today, Gideon?" I asked as I removed my boots and coat.

My uncle's roommate brightened. "I'm gaining." He gently touched his ribs. "The pain is better."

"We had a foot of new snow last night. And I was happy this morning to have a car with front-wheel drive," I said conversationally.

"Wally told me it was snowing when came by to see me last night."

Exasperation welled up inside of me. "I asked him to meet me at the house yesterday, and he never showed up."

"He said to tell you he had a job interview."

I made a face. I'd never heard of job interviews that early in the morning. I didn't say anything.

"Wally told me we were out of garbage bags. In Watertown, we're required to purchase them from the city. I gave him the $20 you left with me for a haircut."

"What?" I struggled to control my anger. That sleazebag! He had put Charlie on the spot, knowing full well the old man was conscientious about things he was responsible for. I doubted Wally would buy trash bags with my $20. I took a deep breath. "I can give you another twenty."

Charlie was silent for a moment as if choosing his words carefully. "You better keep your money. If my hairdresser comes by, she knows I'm good for the cash. And there's one more thing. The title for the car is in your aunt's desk. I'd rather not leave it there, just in case, and I'd like my wristwatch."

I wished he had thought of the title and his watch yesterday when we were at the house, but he clearly didn't trust Wally or Verna any more than I was learning to. "Okay. I'll call over there and arrange to pick them up this afternoon."

The phone in the room rang, and I answered it.

"It's Allen. I'm just calling to see if you arrived at the hospital safely."

"Thank you, I did."

"Is there anything I can do to help you out today?"

"Charlie wants me to get the title to his car. I'm going to go by his house this afternoon."

"Why don't I come with you? While we're there, we'll look over the furniture that belongs to Charlie. If he goes to the place in Ogdensburg, he'll need to get his things out of the house."

"That would be great. Charlie and I will practice walking this morning. Could we meet there at about one? I'll call the house. I suspect Verna is still there."

"I'll see you at one."

I hung up and called the Washington Street house.

"What do you want?" Verna demanded.

It was on the tip of my tongue to ask what Verna was still doing there, but instead, I took a second to calm myself before explaining. "I need to get a couple of things for Charlie. He is walking each day, and if he passes the mobility test, he'll be going to the assisted-living facility in Ogdensburg. He won't be able to pay the upkeep of the house and the costs of his continuing care. We'll remove his possessions from the house preparatory to turning it over to Wally. I'd like to assess what needs to be moved."

"I guess it's all right," she said begrudgingly.

"We'll be there at one."

After I hung up, I turned to Charlie. "Let's practice walking?"

He put his feet over the side of the bed. "I'd better, although I'm not feeling very good."

His color did seem off. Odd, since he had seemed okay when I arrived. I guessed that telling me about Wally's visit and overhearing my call to Verna had upset him. I probably should have called Verna from the waiting room.

I helped him into his robe and placed the walker beside him. He was wearing the bed socks that hospital patients wear. I removed them and got him into his bedroom slippers. He shakily stood, and then fell backward, collapsing onto the bed. His face was ashen and he gasped for breath.

Between gasps, he mumbled. "I'm in terrible pain."

My heart seemed to drop into my stomach. I buzzed for the nurse. When no one appeared, I ran into the hall and grabbed the first nurse I saw.

"I need your help. My uncle is having some kind of spell!"

The nurse rushed into Charlie's room. Moments later, another nurse came running. I stood by helplessly while they checked his vital signs. He continued gasping for breath. From my experience as a hospice volunteer, I suspected he was having Chain-Stokes breathing, a usual preliminary to death. My knees felt weak. I pulled a chair close to Charlie's bed and gratefully sat.

"Perhaps you should call his minister," Gideon suggested.

I turned to Gideon. "Charlie is still a member of the Baptist Church on Public Square."

"I'll make the call for you from the waiting room."

"Thanks, I don't want to leave Charlie's side just now." I was convinced Charlie was dying, and it seemed Gideon thought so too.

"I want to tell you," Charlie said between gasps, "how much I loved your dad." His breathing grew more labored as if trying to talk had been too much for him.

I struggled to keep back tears. How should I respond? Was Charlie already passing in and out, between this world and the next? "I miss him, too. Say hello for me when you see him, and I hope that won't be anytime soon."

Gideon returned to the room. "The church is sending someone over. He should be here within the hour."

"Thanks, Gideon." Tears leaks from my eyes. I found a tissue in my purse, wiped my eyes, and blew my nose." I'll just sit here beside my uncle until the minister comes."

Charlie's labored breathing grew no worse, but he was whiter than the bedsheets. I fought back tears and tried to pray. Why at such times were prayers so elusive? Is it that grief overwhelms our ability to form words? Possibly that's one reason why hymns are so powerful. They provide words for deep feeling when no words are forthcoming.

Forty-five, long minutes passed before a short, balding minister from the First Baptist Church entered the room.

"I'm Pastor Dallas Walker." He held out a hand.

I introduced myself and shook his hand. "My uncle, Charlie Hall, has taken a turn. We're really worried." I turned to Charlie, trying to keep my voice from shaking. "I'll walk down the hall and give you a few minutes alone together, ok?" He nodded.

My knees felt weak as I made my way to the waiting room. It was empty, and I collapsed into a stained, upholstered chair, covered my face with my hands, and sobbed, overcome by the possibility of losing my beloved uncle. Crying left me feeling desiccated, as dry and hollow as bones. Had I expected my intervention could prevent the inevitable?

I sniffled, blew my nose, and straightened my back, thinking of Dad. He liked women, but had little experience with them. As a child, he had treated me the same way as my brother. Yet as I became a young woman, he was less sure what to do. And I supposed the predictable result was that I thought I failed to measure up to his male standards of behavior. Now, with a sudden flash of insight, I knew that I was more like him than I realized. The steel in my spine came from him. He'd approve of the firm stand I'd taken with the greedy relatives.

When I returned to the room, the minister was praying. I stood in the doorway and bowed my head. If faith was what was left when you had nothing else, why did the pastor's words seem as dry and hollow as I was feeling?

When the pastor finished, my uncle's face was still drained of color and his breathing remained labored. If the prayers were meant to bring peace to Charlie, I didn't think they'd done so. I thanked the minister for coming and took my place at my uncle's side.

"The pains in my stomach are awful," he said, struggling to get the words out.

"I'm so sorry." I shook my head, my heart aching. What, if anything, could I do? Where was Charlie's doctor? Should I have her paged?

Time passed. He didn't die. However, his condition was miserable enough that I didn't want to leave him. I called Allen from the phone in the room.

"Charlie has taken a turn for the worse. The doctor hasn't been in, and I want to be here when she arrives. Would you mind going by Washington Street without me to get the title for his car?"

Allen didn't ask any questions. I suspected he had gathered from the urgency in my voice that his friend's hold on life was tenuous. "I'll come by the hospital when I've gotten the title."

"Thanks, Allen. I'll see you in a bit."

It seemed like forever before the doctor arrived, and it wasn't Charlie's regular doctor. The doctor on call, a tired-looking man with a receding hairline looked more like a car salesman than a physician. He introduced himself as Dr. Colman. I retreated while he examined his patient, then I returned. "What's going on?" Charlie asked.

The doctor seemed to think for a minute. "I'm not sure. I'll give you pain medication and order an endoscopy as soon as it can be arranged." He scribbled notes on his clipboard and prepared to leave. I followed him into the hall. "I don't understand. I've never known my uncle to have any digestive problems."

"He's an old man." Dr. Colman scanned the printout on his clipboard. "It says here Mr. Hall is 87."

"My uncle has had asthma for years, but aside from that, he's been really healthy."

The doctor shrugged. "I'll see if I can get to the bottom of what's ailing him." His manner and tone of voice didn't reassure me.

After Charlie got the pain medication, he fell asleep. It made me angry that pain medications were doled out sparingly for someone his age. It was unlikely that he, who would only reluctantly take a drink at holiday time and then nurse it for hours, would become a dope addict. I sat beside his bed too upset to read or chat with Gideon, who had returned to the room as soon as the pastor left.

It was after three when Allen arrived, looking as pleased as a little boy who had just caught a fish. He handed me Charlie's watch and the title to the car.

"*That woman* is clearly still staying in Charlie's house. She didn't want to let me in. But I took the precaution of going there with my friend, Deputy-Sheriff Albright. She had to then."

I shook my head in wonderment and managed a smile. "Allen, you surely know how to get things done."

He nodded toward Charlie, who was still asleep. "How is he?"

"He's been really in bad shape today, and the doctor can't seem to figure out why."

"I'll check in with you both tomorrow." He left with the self-satisfied look still on his face.

In the late afternoon, before Charlie woke up, I reluctantly left the hospital. The roads were slippery and I drove slowly. There was more traffic than usual, and I remembered it was Friday. The weekend was coming. The test the doctor said he would order probably wouldn't be done until Monday. By next week, it might not be necessary. It didn't look like Charlie was going to live, let alone move to Ogdensburg. If he did, he'd probably be going to a nursing home instead of the nice assisted-living facility near his daughter. And Verna still hadn't vacated the Washington Street house.

Chapter 16

Saturday, February 12, 1994

To my relief, Charlie was awake when I arrived at his room the next morning. He still looked pale and wan, and he winced as he shifted position in the bed. His breakfast tray lay unopened beside the bed. "Can I help you with your breakfast?" I asked.

"I can't eat."

"How about a few sips of juice?"

Charlie shook his head. "It hurts too much when I take something."

"You haven't had anything since yesterday. And darn little before that." I regretted that I'd not quizzed him about what he had eaten before coming to the hospital. Now didn't seem the best time to do so.

Gideon spoke up. "They gave Charlie a few sips of water with his mediations and he couldn't keep it down."

"Oh, I see."

"Since your uncle is awake, and I'm going to be released later today, perhaps we should have a short prayer service," Gideon suggested.

"What do you say, Charlie?"

He nodded, although not enthusiastically.

Gideon took his Bible from the bedside table and handed it to me. "Phyllis, I'd like you to read Charlie something. Your uncle has difficulty hearing me."

I wasn't aware that Charlie had hearing problems. I was soft-spoken, and he could hear me. Maybe he just resisted being preached to. Having ears but not hearing was a biblical reference in both the Old and New Testaments.

"Psalm 43," Gideon announced.

Charlie interrupted, "Could you please read Psalm 23?"

"That's the psalm for the dead," Gideon said.

"Charlie, do you really want me to read that?"

"No." There was a hint of resentment in his voice. He closed his eyes.

I was convinced that he really wanted to die.

I began to read:

> Vindicate me, my God, and plead my cause against an
> unfaithful nation.
> Rescue me from those who are deceitful and wicked.
> You are my God's stronghold. Why have you rejected me?
> Why must I go about mourning? Oppressed by the enemy?
> Send me your light and your faithful care, let them lead me,
> let them bring me to your Holy Mountain; to the place
> where you dwell.

I continued to read, confident that Gideon had chosen the right psalm.

When I finished, Gideon spoke up. "I'll say a few words and ask you to repeat them."

"When God sends us suffering, he needs to teach us something," I repeated his words. "Let us pray." We bowed our heads. "Help us to walk with Him. Give us strength and courage."

Gideon's words were simple, but the psalm and the prayer couldn't have been more appropriate.

Charlie stirred restlessly for a few moments and then slept.

I pulled up a chair close to Gideon's bed. The psalm and the little sermon had made me confident I was doing the right thing. "That was perfect," I whispered.

"I hope it helped. Psalm 43 has helped me, time and time again."

"I'm not surprised that the hospital is sending you home. They don't keep you a minute longer than is necessary these days."

"They told me I have to rest, but as soon as I'm out of here, I'll visit my wife at Henry Keep Home. I haven't been there for several days."

"I'm sorry about your wife, Gideon. I've been so immersed in my uncle's problems, that's all I've thought about." In the many hours I had been in the hospital, I'd seen no one visit this dear old man. He had mentioned supporting his family, but no family was in evidence. Something told me that the missing child or children were a source of great sadness for

118

Gideon. Perhaps something more painful to remember than his war experiences.

"There's an upside to my wife's condition. She now has dementia and probably doesn't miss me when I don't go."

"How often do you visit?"

"About every day. And I've come to realize the visits are more for me than for her. She doesn't always recognize me." His eyes were sad. "I was on my way there when I fell on the ice."

Dr. Colman came in to talk with Gideon.

I rose. "Goodbye, Gideon. It's been a real pleasure to get to know you."

"I'm sorry for your uncle," he whispered.

"I know. But you've done what you could to help. Thank you for that." I took his transparent, blue-veined hand and gave it a gentle squeeze.

That evening, I told Agnes about the impromptu religious service. She had been a staunch Catholic for many years, and in her own way, very religious.

"I've been saying my rosary for your uncle. I'm pleased, but not surprised, that there is someone in the same room to give him spiritual comfort."

"Sadly, Gideon is going home today."

"What about Charlie's pastor?"

"I guess I didn't tell you that he is in such bad shape his pastor visited yesterday."

"I know about those visits. Sometimes when a priest comes to give the last rites to a person, it's a bit like the dessert after a meal. When it is finished, it's a signal to the dinner guests that it's time to go."

"On the other hand, when my father-in-law was near death, the family was called in," I said. "To everyone's surprise he rallied, if only for a few days."

"That's one thing that makes navigating the end of a life so difficult. Everyone is different. What works for one may bring about the death of another."

"I'm afraid my uncle lost the will to live some time ago. Losing Miriam, the pressure put on him by Wally and Verna, and being sick have all taken their toll. I don't think he's going to make it."

Dear Agnes went to the cupboard and took out a bottle of sherry and two sherry glasses. "I've been saving this for medicinal purposes," she said with a twinkle of sad understanding in her eyes.

Chapter 17

Sunday, February 13, 1994

When I spoke with my husband last night, he encouraged me to go to church with Agnes. I must have sounded pretty upset on the phone, since it had been years since I had been a regular churchgoer. But my place was at Charlie's side, so soon after breakfast, I left for the hospital.

It was one of those North Country mornings where the sky and the snow are the same pewter color. The bright lights of the hospital dispelled a bit of the gloom that seemed to permeate everything.

The social worker, Jeannette Doney, signaled to me as I walked by her door and indicated the vacant chair across from her desk. I took off my scarf and gloves and loosened my coat.

"Mr. Hall's condition has worsened. He hasn't eaten anything or had any fluid in days. Perhaps it's time he went to a nursing home."

"If he is in such a dire condition, maybe he should stay in the hospital." It occurred me to that Charlie might be sent to a nursing home to die.

Jeannette Doney slowly shook her head. "Family members are often one step behind the curve as far as what care is needed. Our recommendation is for a nursing home."

I gathered from her firm tone of voice that Charlie's fate had already been decided. "When will he be released from the hospital?"

"Dr. Panbehchi spoke with Dr. Colman, who has ordered one more test. He'll have that Monday. And if it shows nothing treatable, he'll be released as soon as we find him a nursing-home placement."

"Thanks for the head's up. If you tell me what's available, I'll check out the places today and tomorrow."

"I'm afraid at the moment the only available bed is at Angel Inn."

I stood. "Will you please call them and explain that I will drop by there today?"

"Sure, it shouldn't be any problem. There's a supervisor there at all times. Here's a Xerox with the directions." She handed me the paper. "I can imagine you are disappointed since you hoped he wouldn't have to go to a nursing home."

"Yes, but I understand my uncle's condition. And he's very depressed. Going to a nursing home probably will send him farther down that road."

My heart was heavy as I made my way to Charlie's room. He was asleep. To my surprise, Gideon was still in the room and Allen was waiting to see me. He was dressed in his Sunday best, including a wide tie popular in the 1970s. He had shaved and looked quite spiffy. He tipped his hat as he always did when he met me—a holdover from a bygone era.

"May I speak with you alone?" he asked.

I went with him to the waiting room. "What is on your mind, Allen?"

"When I was sixteen years old, I was a fireman on the railroad. I worked my way to Winnipeg. When I crossed back into the US, I had only one dime. I know what it is like to be far from home and low on cash. If you need a loan…."

I was genuinely touched. He had apparently noticed that the car rental was over $300. "Thank you, Allen. How kind of you. But I'm all set."

"Well, I wanted to make sure. I'm been concerned. I'm off to spend time with my wife and cousin."

I walked with him to the elevator, and then returned to Charlie's room.

"Why are you still here?" I whispered to Gideon.

"I had a reaction to the medicine they are giving me, and they decided to keep me here another day."

"How are you feeling now?"

"Weak, but better."

Charlie stirred, and I went to his side.

"I'm in terrible pain," he murmured.

"I'll talk to the nurse and get you something."

I found the nurse, a young woman wearing thick glasses.

"My uncle, Charlie Hall, in room 302 is in pain. I know from being a hospice volunteer that people don't need to be in pain at the end of life." I surprised myself at the authority in my voice.

"Of course. I'll check to see if I can give him something, or call his doctor."

I returned to Charlie's room. Thankfully, he had nodded off again.

I settled into a chair, took a book from my handbag, and opened it. I stared at the words as if they were a foreign language. Time passed slowly. I dreaded having to tell Charlie about the nursing home, and I kept thinking of all that needed to be done if he gave up his Washington Street house.

He woke again, grimacing in pain.

I went to his side. "Charlie, I hate to have to tell you this, but the social worker told me that if you don't pick up, you'll need to go to a nursing home. She's arranging for me to stop by Angel Inn and look at it. It's the only bed available."

"I just want to die," he said.

I looked from Charlie to Gideon.

"It is Sunday," Gideon said. "And we should have another little service. I'd like you to read the third chapter of Job."

Charlie stirred uncomfortably, but didn't object.

I took the Bible again, found the chapter, and pulled a chair close to Charlie's bed. I began to read:

After this opened Job his mouth, and cursed his day. And Job spake, and said, 'Let the day perish wherein I was born, and the night in which I was conceived.'

I found the text difficult to read, but I continued reading the grim lament with its longing for the release of death:

There the wicked cease from troubling and the weary be at rest…. The small and great are there, and the servant is free from his master. Wherefore is light given to him that is in misery and life unto the bitter in soul which long for death, but it cometh not, and dig for it more than treasure, which rejoice exceedingly, and are glad when they can find the grave?

Despite the archaic language, the passage accurately described my uncle's state of mind. He longed for death.

"I'm going to preach a little sermon," Gideon said. "And Phyllis, will you repeat my words again?"

"Of course." I couldn't read Charlie's face, and I wasn't sure what he thought about what was going on. But what could it hurt?

Gideon began in the cadenced voice he used from the pulpit. "I want to recall to you Job's story. He was a wealthy man with a large family and many flocks. Job was blameless and upright, avoiding evil and doing good."

I repeated his words and waited for the next.

"In one day, God allowed Satan to take everything away, wealth, flocks, children, and servants. Still, Job praised God, and then Satan afflicted Job with terrible boils. So, Job fell from wealth and health to misery."

Gideon took a breath and continued. "Job questioned God's justice and wanted to die. But through it all, Job's life belonged to God."

I wasn't sure I was able to do justice to Gideon's eloquence, but I did my best to recreate the poignancy of his heartfelt words. "By despairing, Job was siding with the Devil. Job wanted to die, but Job's life belonged to God. And by wanting to die, Job was denying God."

Gideon was done, and I swallowed before speaking. "Thank you, Gideon," I managed to say, giving him back his Bible.

The old preacher's sermon had moved me, and I felt a difference. Perhaps it was grace. Perhaps it was the presence of God. Whatever it was, whether or not it helped Charlie, it had touched me, somehow restored me.

The nurse arrived, breaking the spell we seemed to be under. She had a pill for Charlie.

"Maybe you will be able to rest easy for a while Mr. Hall," she said.

I collected my things. "Charlie, I'm off to take a look at Angel Inn."

Driving to the nursing home, I experienced a sense of peace I hadn't felt before. Perhaps it wasn't up to me to fix everything, to save Charlie's life, to save him from predatory relatives. Maybe in my stress, I was denying God, too. Nothing had changed as a result of Gideon's preaching, but everything had changed. It was as if heaven and earth came close, if only for a few moments, and now I was able to move forward without the terrible anxiety that had made the last days so difficult.

This morning wasn't the first time I experienced a transcendent experience, the peace beyond all understanding.

Always my rational mind discounted them and swept such experiences under the rug of reason. Today, reason warred with experience, and experience won. The anxiety that had weighed me down since I got Jill's call dissipated. I would do what I could for Charlie, but I couldn't control life and death or the actions of other people

Angel Inn was on a residential street, not far from Brookside Cemetery. It was a disorderly sprawl of buildings, painted white with green shutters. It had apparently been a home that had been added on to and converted into a nursing facility. Out in front, a bathtub stood on one end. The inside of the bathtub was painted blue as a background for a statute of the Virgin Mary.

Inside, I took the tour and didn't care for the frilly, tied-back curtains on many of the windows. I almost expected to see doilies on the backs of the chairs in the sitting room. Yet, the place was clean, and the staff apparently competent. The facility smelled of Lysol instead of urine. It would do. At least, it wasn't Whispering Pines.

That evening, Agnes had a boiled dinner with Ben and Jerry's Chunky Monkey ice cream for the dessert. It was the first time I had Ben and Jerry's. I was always watching my weight, and on several occasions, I'd studied the calorie count on the rich ice cream. But tonight, I didn't care how many calories I was eating. The enormity of death made such things seem insignificant. As I ate, I kept wondering if I should be in the hospital by Charlie's side. He could be actively dying while I was enjoying a good dinner and eating ice cream.

Chapter 18

Monday, February 14, 1994, Valentine's Day

Six inches of powdery fresh snow fell during the night, and now the gray landscape was white again in the morning sunshine. The hospital auxiliary was selling carnations at the front entrance to the hospital. I bought two, one for Charlie, the other for Gideon. I put my nose into them and inhaled their sweet smell.

To my surprise, Charlie was sitting up in his bed. His color was good, and he was alert. He seemed much better. Gideon, fully dressed, awaiting his release, sat in one of the two chairs.

"Well, look at you two, all bright-eyed and bushy-tailed," I said. "Happy Valentine's Day." The irony of wishing these two men who had lost loved ones Happy Valentine's Day didn't prevent me from smiling cheerfully. I gave them their carnations and helped pin the flowers on.

"I started feeling better last night," Charlie said. "I sat up for a while, and I had a little beef broth. And this morning, I had scrambled eggs and some Cheerios."

If he had told me that he'd gone dancing the night before, I wouldn't have been more surprised. He had eaten well after not being able to eat for days.

"Will you be up for walking later on?"

Charlie's face lit up like it did the first day I arrived. "I'll give it a try."

"Good. We'll see what the doctor has to say."

"She's already been in."

"I'd like to talk with her," I said. "If you could stay a couple more days, you might qualify for United Helpers in Ogdensburg. And that would mean you wouldn't have to move twice."

"She's probably still somewhere around. She wasn't in long ago."

"I'll see if I can find her."

I left the room and headed to the nurse's station. The nurse on duty looked up. She was the same woman whom I had summoned when Charlie had his spell.

"Good morning. Happy Valentine's Day."

"Thank you," the nurse said with a bright smile. "What can I help you with?"

"Is Dr. Panbehchi still around? I want to talk with her."

"The doctor just went into room 309. If you wait near there, you might catch her between patients."

"I'll do that."

I lingered near Room 309, trying to look nonchalant. I was still wearing my heavy coat and boots. Fortunately, I was there only minutes before Dr. Panbehchi emerged from the room.

"May I please speak with you about my uncle, Charlie Hall? I'm wondering if you have gotten the results of his tests."

"Yes, and we found nothing. We'll be releasing him tomorrow."

"He seems to have turned the corner. He told me he ate something last night and again this morning, and he's sitting up."

"I started him on Prozac on Friday. That probably explains his turnaround."

"Would the Prozac work that quickly?" I remembered that each time my mother had bouts of depression it had taken three weeks for an antidepressant to kick in."

"Yes. It could."

"Is it possible he could stay a few more days in the hospital to regain his strength and begin walking again? That way he wouldn't have to move twice."

"I'm sorry." The doctor shook her head sympathetically. "We need his bed. We're full up right now. There's a lot of flu around."

I headed back to Charlie's room, deep in thought. I didn't know whether his sudden improvement was due to Gideon's sermon or the result of the Prozac. But I couldn't help but feel it had been Gideon's preaching that had made the essential difference, because it had to me.

Back in his room, I dreaded telling Charlie the news.

"The doctor is sending you to a nursing home tomorrow," I said. "But I hope you will stay there only temporarily."

He smiled. "So do I."

I noted that he had not said he wanted to die yet today. "You'll need to work on your walking."

Later that morning, when Charlie was back in bed, exhausted after his walk, a nurse came in with a wheelchair and Gideon's discharge instructions. The nurse read over his instructions and then helped him into the wheelchair.

"We'll miss you, Gideon," I said. "It's been lovely getting to know you." I wanted to say more, but didn't find the words. What had happened when he preached was unexplainable, irrational, but very special.

A look passed between us, and I realized that words weren't necessary.

"It's been my pleasure."

"Stay well. And be careful on the ice."

I experienced a wave of regret that I wouldn't be seeing Gideon again. He was one of those exceptional people who come into your life and you never forget.

"All the best, Gideon," Charlie said.

We watched as the nurse rolled Gideon out of the room and into the hall, out of our lives.

"There's one thing I'd like for you to do right away," Charlie said.

"What's so urgent?"

"I'd like you to get my gun out of the Washington Street house."

My jaw dropped. "Gun?"

Chapter 19

I'd forgotten that my gun is still there. I was a good shot and a member of the Troopers' competitive pistol team. When I retired from the State Police, I bought the Colt 38 Police Special that I'd used all those years. I don't think we should leave it in the house. You better have Allen go with you."

"Where is it?"

"It's in the closet in a box with some other Trooper things. It's on the top shelf, way in the back, behind a box of camera equipment."

I was still nonplussed. "What will I do with it once I get it?"

"Turn it in at the sheriff's office. And while you're getting the gun, in the same box is a Masonic book. I'd like you to bring that to me."

The Masonic Order probably had some secret passwords or handshakes or something. And to a Mason, the material in it was as loaded as a gun. Charlie probably wanted to destroy it or give it to a member of the brotherhood.

"I'll call Allen and see if he'll help." After the problems I'd already had with Verna and Wally, I was afraid the presence of a gun could escalate things all out of proportion. I had to get it out of the house as soon as possible.

I called Allen from the waiting room and arranged to meet him at the house at two. I also called Verna to tell her we were coming to the house, but there was no answer and no answering machine.

I arrived at the house at two, and Allen was there waiting by a red pickup truck. He wasn't alone.

"Phyllis, this is Paul Versneider," Allen said. "He sometimes does a little work for me."

Paul, a muscular young man about 6'2" and in his early 20s, smelled vaguely of manure and hay.

"Nice to meet you, Paul," I said.

Paul grinned. One of his front teeth was broken. "I've done a lot of things for Allen, but this is my first time being a bodyguard."

"I hope you haven't come in vain. I've called the house several times, but no one answers."

Allen's eyes brightened, and he seemed pleased with himself. "There's one set of footprints going in, and none coming out."

I smiled and shook my head. "I can see you haven't forgotten your police training."

I went to the front door, rang the bell, and then knocked loudly.

It was several minutes before Wally opened the door. His hair wasn't combed, and he could use a shave. He was groggy as if he'd just woken up. I caught a whiff of something that I remembered from my college days. Wally had been smoking marihuana.

"You woke me up," he complained.

I wanted to ask what he was doing sleeping at my uncle's house, but didn't. "I called, but no one answered. We're here to get Charlie's gun. He wants it out of the house."

Wally's face registered confusion, but he stood aside to let us in.

"Paul, go with Phyllis," Allen said. "I'll stay down here with Wally."

Wally opened his mouth to object, but closed it again. We wiped our feet on the doormat but didn't remove our boots.

Paul followed me up the stairs and then stood in the doorway to my uncle's room. I found the box exactly where Charlie had said it would be. Inside was a box of cartridges, a few photos, a State Police tie clip, a small leather-bound book with the Masonic symbol on the cover, and something neatly wrapped in a cloth. I removed the cloth that smelled of gun oil and gingerly took out the revolver. It was cold to my touch and heavy. I didn't know much about guns, but the 38 looked like Charlie had kept it in good condition.

"I've found everything my uncle wants," I told Paul.

"A piece of cake," Paul chortled.

"We're not out of here yet," I whispered.

"Yeah, that guy looks pretty rough, but he doesn't look very tough."

I nodded my head in agreement and followed Paul down the stairs.

Allen was in the hallway with Wally, watching us descend.

"You've taken something else," Wally said accusingly.

"Yes, Charlie wanted a Masonic book." I held it up.

"This is my house," he said belligerently.

My temper flared. "Not yet it isn't. I'm changing the locks. I don't want you here, disturbing my uncle's things." I hadn't intended to charge the locks, but once I'd said it, I realized it would be the only way to get Wally and Verna out of the house.

"Charlie's things are shit," Wally said.

"They're still his things. This is still his house. So, I want you out of here within the hour."

"Verna still has stuff here."

"Well then, you better contact her. I'll have a locksmith here as soon as I can arrange it."

I turned to Allen. "Where's the nearest locksmith?"

"On the Square. I can show you where it is."

Outside, Allen chuckled. "You're your father's daughter, no doubt about that. The good thing is, you don't look like him."

It was true. I had spoken with authority about changing the locks, just as my father would have done.

I smiled. "I'll take that as a compliment. Thanks for your support, Paul."

Allen took off his baseball cap and ran a hand through his hair. "Phyllis, now we have to turn the gun into the sheriff's office. I'll go with you and take you to the locksmith. After that, you can drop me at home."

Allen shook Paul's hand, and the young man got into his truck. I still held the gun and book. Driving through the city with the gun in hand didn't seem like a good idea. I crammed it into my handbag. Great. Now it was a concealed weapon. I got into my uncle's car and put my purse and the Masonic book on the back seat. What was I doing in this godforsaken place with a gun in my purse?

Chapter 20

The county sheriff's office was on the other side of town, about twenty minutes away. It seemed like it took us forever to get there. The woman at the desk of the new, two-story building directed us to the office of Undersheriff Jim Lafferty. I uneasily clutched my purse with its concealed weapon, unsure what to expect.

Undersheriff Lafferty was a big, formidable-looking man probably in his early fifties with a short, military-style haircut. He wore a blue police uniform and when he rose from his desk to greet us, I noted the highly polished shoes and knife-sharp crease in his pants. He reminded me of my dad and all the Troopers I had known.

"Allen, good to see you." The officer shook his hand.

"Jim, this is Phyllis Haislip. She's Charlie Hall's niece and Addison Hall's daughter," Allen said.

"Pleased to meet you," the undersheriff said. "Have a chair, Mrs. Haislip. I knew your dad when he was stationed in Watertown. He had such a fine reputation that local folks wanted him to run for sheriff. And your uncle stops in to visit once in a blue moon. What can I do for you?"

I took a deep breath. I vaguely remembered Dad talking about running for sheriff and deciding not to. I explained about Charlie's gun and gingerly removed it from my purse.

Undersheriff Lafferty smiled. "We'll be glad to help. We'll keep it for you for a year. Any time you want it, just contact me."

Relief seemed to flow out my fingertips as I handed him the gun. He was probably relieved too, that I wasn't reporting a crime.

He turned it in his hands. "That's a real antique. It was one good gun."

We exchanged pleasantries for a few minutes. I had gotten used to the slow pace of life in the area. Instead of the small talk annoying me, it seemed comforting, just right, allowing me to reestablish my equanimity.

Back in the car, Allen directed us to the locksmith. I barely saw the snowy streets we passed through. Changing the locks was a big step, even though I felt sure it was the thing to do.

The locksmith was a slightly built man with olive skin and dark eyes, magnified by thick glasses. His small cluttered shop was long and narrow, reminding me of a shoebox. He went through the *who do you know that I know* drill. When that was over, I explained that I wanted new locks on my uncle's house at 102 Washington Street as soon as possible.

The locksmith looked at his watch. "I can't do it today, but I'll be there at ten tomorrow morning."

Allen helped me select new locks, and I paid for them. "I recall there were Halls that lived in Carthage," the locksmith said.

"That might have been us," I said. "It was a long time ago though. We lived in West Carthage from 1945 to 1955."

I felt exhausted when we left the locksmith's store. Back in the car, I asked, "Allen, could you meet me at the house tomorrow morning to make sure there's no funny business with the locksmith?"

"Of course. I'll be there. Shall I ask Paul to come along?"

"I don't think that will be necessary, since we got the gun out of the house."

Allen took off his cap and ran his fingers through his white hair. I had come to realize he did that whenever he was thinking deeply about something.

"First thing in the morning, we'll go by the hospital. We need to make you Charlie's power of attorney. Changing the locks could be questioned."

"Good. I've had it with Wally and Verna. Getting a power of attorney never occurred to me, but that will give me the legal right to change the locks."

"Who is his lawyer?"

"His name is Oliver Wisner.'"

Allen thought for a moment. "I'll call my attorney today. It shouldn't be a problem. Those kinds of documents are pretty standard. I can pick it up tomorrow morning on the way to the hospital."

"But if Charlie signs it, won't it have to be in the presence of a notary?"

"No problem. I'm the oldest notary in Jefferson County."

I gave him an appreciative look. "Allen, you never cease to amaze me."

I dropped Allen at his house and returned to the hospital. Charlie was sitting up in bed. Gideon's bed was still empty. This made me wonder if the hospital was really full or if this was just an excuse to move Charlie to a nursing home.

I told him that Verna was still in the house and about my confrontation with Wally.

"We've got to get those people out of the house. I'm getting the locks changed. And to do that, I'll need a power of attorney. Allen will come by with the documents tomorrow morning. Once we've changed the locks, you would be able to return there when you are able if you'd like."

Charlie let out a long breath. "I'd still have to deal with them. And I don't care if I never see either of them again."

"Okay, it's your call."

"What's next?"

"I haven't thought all that through yet. I wasn't sure you wanted to give up the house. Since you don't want to return there, we'll need to get your things out of the house preliminary to turning it over to Wally."

"And you'll have to cancel all the services, like the utilities, that I've been paying for."

"I've got my work cut out for me." I stood. "We'll be here tomorrow morning, probably about nine."

On the way to Carthage, I stopped at a Rite-Aid pharmacy and bought Agnes a two-pound box of Valentine candy. While we ate dinner and sampled the chocolates, I filled her in on my nerve-racking day.

After dinner, I called home to wish my husband Happy Valentine's Day. He and Alex had taken a balloon and a Valentine card over to my mom. Otis assured me that we would celebrate Valentine's Day on my return.

"I'm not sure when that will be. I don't feel I've worn out my welcome at Agnes's, but I just want to come home."

"Do what you have to do," Otis said. "Alex and I are doing okay."

"One more thing. Are my daffodils blooming?"

"There's been a cold snap here, and the few that came out are hanging their heads."

"I know how they feel. If you pick them, bring them into the house and put them in water, they may recover."

Otis laughed. "I'm about as good with daffodils as I am with dinners."

I smiled. Otis didn't cook at all. I hung up the phone and sat for a few minutes on the small painted chair near the telephone, filled with longing for Otis and Alex. For home.

Agnes, who had been politely watching television in the living room, came to join me. "You've had a very stressful day and we both ate a lot of chocolates. What do you say we go out for a walk?"

I was incredulous. "It's cold out there and dark. Is it safe?"

"The sidewalks are clear and it's a beautiful night."

Agnes thought the snow was beautiful, too.

"Only if you take my arm. You may not be afraid of falling, but I'll be wearing my plastic boots."

We put on our winter gear and stepped out into the darkness. It was a clear night with no moon. The stars were brilliant, like crystals of glittering ice. There was no wind and no sound except our footsteps. We walked arm-in-arm in the frosty air, soaking in the peace and vastness of the night sky.

Too soon, we were back at Agnes's house and thoughts of what lay ahead crowded in. I would have difficulty sleeping again tonight. I had been getting so little sleep, I worried about sustaining the equanimity that I strove to maintain in spite of how upset I felt. Since I had been planning only to stay the weekend, I hadn't packed more than three-days' supply of my medications, including sleeping pills. Like many women my age, I was undergoing hormone replacement therapy. Lack of medicines wasn't fatal. Yet, I recalled the t-shirts with the statement. "I am out of estrogen and I have a gun." I no longer had a gun; but hot flashes and night sweats contributed to my stressed-induced sleeplessness.

Chapter 21

The next morning was the first day since my arrival that the temperature was above freezing, and I hadn't worn my boots. I heard snowmelt running into the drains in the hospital parking lot when I got out of the car. There were puddles everywhere, and hard patches of ice that would probably still be in place in April. I cautiously maneuvered through the morass to the hospital entrance.

Allen stood in Charlie's room, holding a sheaf of papers that would make me power of attorney.

"I've got everything we need here," he said.

"Well done," I said.

"And I've brought my seal to notarize them." He placed the papers on the over-the-bed rolling table in front of Charlie.

My uncle signed them, and Allen notarized them.

"They are kicking me out of here," Charlie said.

143

"When?" I asked.

"They'll discharge me sometime this morning, and an ambulance will take me to the nursing home. So, I'll be settling in there by the time you're through with the locksmith."

I hesitated. "Do you need me to go with you?"

"I should be okay."

"I'll drop by to see you later."

"Wally came by to see me last night," Charlie said. "He brought me a photo that Miriam had blown up and framed. It's over there by the door."

I hadn't noticed the large picture on the floor when I entered the room, so intent had I been on the business at hand. Now I examined it. The photograph was of Charlie, handsome and proud in the glory of his young manhood. He wore his State Police uniform with its broad-brimmed hat. Sitting astride a big horse, he looked like a Hollywood cowboy or a medieval knight.

"The original picture was taken at the State Fair in Syracuse, and it appeared in the Syracuse paper," he explained.

"It's a grand picture," I said.

"I'd like you to have it."

"I'd love it, but isn't it something you want to keep?"

Charlie made a dismissive motion with one hand. "Miriam liked it, but it makes me uneasy."

I wasn't sure where he was coming from with this. Perhaps he didn't want to be reminded of how Miriam had fed his vanity.

"Thanks. I'll treasure it."

"Wally told me you were going to change the locks, and he wants a key to the house."

Allen shook his head. "He can't be serious."

"That isn't all," Charlie said. "Wally told me he needed more garbage bags. He was looking for another handout. That's probably why he brought me the photo. I'm glad you didn't leave me any money."

"Well, I suspect he wanted to clean up a bit of the mess in the house before we kicked him out," I said in a half-hearted effort to give Wally the benefit of the doubt.

"I wouldn't count on it," Allen said.

"We have to run," I told Charlie. "The locksmith will be at the house at ten. I want you to be thinking of everything in the house that is yours and not Miriam's."

"Gladly," he said. "There's one thing I particularly want you to have. It's Ellen's family silver. You've eaten off it many a Thanksgiving and Christmas. We always joked because the H initials stood for her family name and not Hall. But the service is sterling silver and should be worth something, over and above the sentimental value."

"I remember four teaspoons that were made by someone in our family, a silversmith in the 1840s. They were in the shape of little shovels, each one made from a silver dollar. As a kid, they always fascinated me. Thank you. I'll take it home with me." I already had my mother's family sterling, but I appreciated his gesture.

"We'd best be on our way," Allen said.

We arrived at the Washington Street house early. Wally's battered Dodge van was in the driveway. I knocked at the front door.

Wally opened it. "We're here to change the locks," I said. "I'm glad you're here, it will make things easier."

The locksmith arrived in his van, got out with his tools, and began to remove the old, front-door lock.

I stood outside with Allen, watching the locksmith work. Wally came out to join us. The eves dripped, and from time to time, large icicles melted enough to fall into adjacent snowbanks with a crash.

"I'm here because I want one of the new keys," Wally said.

It was on the tip of my tongue to say that if he'd turned over the keys before this, changing the locks wouldn't have been necessary.

"You'll have the new keys when the lawyer turns them over to you," I said mildly. "And that should be within a week or so, give or take a few days. An ambulance will be taking Charlie to a nursing home this afternoon.

Wally frowned. "He's pretty sick."

"He'll need around-the-clock care until we're sure he's out of the woods and he's steadier on his feet. When that happens, he'll move to the assisted-living facility in Ogdensburg. He will be giving up the house. Until that time, I expect you to stay out of my uncle's home. We'll be coming to remove his possessions before turning it over to you." I found I liked speaking with authority.

"I want to be here when you take out his things." Wally's tone was challenging as if he expected me to run off with his mother's antiques.

Wally would be hovering about, questioning everything we took from the house. I glanced at Allen, who nodded.

"Fair enough," I said. "I'll call you when we arrange to move his things into storage. It's going to take some time."

The locksmith finished with the front door and went around the back.

"You better get your things," Allen said to Wally. "We'll be locking the place up."

Wally shook his head and rolled his eyes as if to signal that this was all beyond his comprehension. "If you insist."

I was surprised that Wally didn't look happier since clearly, he had wanted Charlie out of the house for some time. Perhaps Wally expected that when Charlie died, he'd get all his things too. The thought crossed my mind that if my uncle had died two weeks ago that might have been the case. But despite all his ailments, he was stronger than Wally and Verna, and whatever they may have done, or not done, to get rid of him.

The locksmith completed his work and left. I put the new keys on Charlie's car keychain, waited for Wally to leave, and locked the doors.

In the car, I sighed with relief. Wally hadn't created a scene.

"I wonder where *that woman* was?" Allen asked.

"I was thinking the same thing. Can it be we are through with her?"

He gave me a disbelieving look. "I doubt it. Let's go look at storage areas."

"I guess that's the next step."

Even though I still needed Allen's help, I felt an urge to say something that would let him ease out of his involvement with my uncle's problems. But I realized that although such words might be appropriate in most cases, they weren't in this. Allen, Charlie, and Dad were buddies in a brotherhood that extended to my uncle's plight and beyond my father's death. There had been much talk in the sixties and seventies about sisterhood. I'd experienced it briefly as a harried graduate-student at Columbia University and later when I became a mother, as if the demands of motherhood allowed me entry into a sisterhood as old as time itself. Now, I was experiencing the enduring strength of the Trooper brotherhood, and was grateful.

Chapter 22

Allen, who seemed to be always one step ahead, had gone by yesterday to check out a storage area on the outskirts of the city where it was handy for soldiers at Fort Drum. There, I rented a 5 by7 foot storage locker in Charlie's name.

"How will we get everything moved?" I asked when we finished.

"I'll call Paul and see when he can help us."

"That would be great. What does Paul do that he can get away in the middle of the week?"

"He has a dairy farm in Croghan. He farms his land and mine. This time of year, he's usually available for a few hours after milking in the morning and before evening chores."

"Shall we aim for tomorrow morning? In the meantime, I'll contact the lawyer to initiate turning over the house to Wally."

"I'll see about getting a truck."

"Thanks, Allen. What would I do without you?"

"Addison's daughter and Charlie's niece. That's a pretty strong pedigree. I'm sure you'd manage fine without me. I'm just glad I'm able to give you a hand. It reminds me of the old days solving problems with your dad. It's been a pleasure."

"I'm glad you're enjoying it. I wish I could say the same." I hadn't mentioned to him my suspicions that Wally and Verna may have done something to harm Charlie. I didn't need to say anything. He had seen enough of them to take their measure, and they hadn't measured up.

We arrived at Allen's house. "You can call the lawyer from my office. That will save you looking for a phone."

"Thanks. I'm not looking forward to seeing the lawyer, but it has to be done. I had dealings with Charlie's lawyer years ago, from a distance, and it wasn't pleasant."

"What was the problem?"

"My cousin's disability made her mother's estate complicated. After my aunt's death, ten years passed, and the lawyer still hadn't settled her estate. In frustration, Charlie called on me for help."

"Oliver Wisner has a reputation in town for dragging things out."

"He only got on with it when I reported him to the New York State Bar's Committee on Ethics. This time around, I anticipate that he will gladly expedite the necessary legal actions to be rid of me, once and for all." I marveled that my actions way back then had been similar to the actions I was taking now. I had acted with authority. How had I forgotten?

"I'll go along with you," Allen offered.

"Thanks. I've no idea what to expect."

In Allen's office, I took off my coat and used the phone to make the appointment to see the lawyer.

"I should call Charlie's neighbor and keep him in the loop," I said when I finished.

"Go right ahead."

I called Ross Moore, expecting to leave a message with his wife. I was surprised to find him at home. I told him what had been going on and about Charlie going to Angel Inn.

"I'm sorry Charlie has to go to a nursing home," Ross said. "But his overall condition will no doubt improve when he gets away from Wally and Verna."

"We hope to remove his things from the house tomorrow."

"You may not be aware that during his marriage to Miriam, your uncle replaced all the appliances in the house. So, in fact, they belong to him."

"I wonder if and when Charlie became aware that Miriam had married him for his steady paycheck."

"He was aware of it, or he wouldn't have told me about buying one appliance after another. I still think he loved Miriam. He just didn't know what he was getting into, especially with her family."

"I know he was very lonely after my aunt died."

"The Maytag dealer here in town buys used appliances. I'll call him if you like."

"I'll speak with Charlie. I suspect he's already concerned about paying for the nursing home. He'll get three weeks covered by Medicare, and I hope his stay there won't be any longer. But at this point, it's hard to know. If he does go into assisted living, that's costly too."

"Charlie has always wanted to pay his own way."

"He's a straight arrow. I'll talk with Charlie this afternoon. Thanks, Ross, for your continued help."

Allen appeared in the doorway with two soft drinks in glass bottles. "What's your pleasure?" He held them out for me to inspect them.

"I've never tried either of them before."

"Neither have I. My granddaughter favors this kind of soda pop, so it must be good."

I realized he must have gotten the soda especially for me. "Thanks, Allen. Managing Charlie's affairs is thirsty business." I took the lime soda.

"I'll try this cherry one." Allen regarded it thoughtfully. "Although I've never much-favored soda pop if there's stronger stuff to drink."

"Yeah, Dad kept a bottle in the cupboard in the kitchen. Sometimes in the evenings after the dishes were done, we'd hear that cupboard door open and shut, and we knew he was having a slug of whiskey." I put down the bottle. "This was good." I looked at my watch and stood. "I'm off to visit Charlie at the nursing home. I'm anxious to find out how he is settling in."

The sunny day made Angle Inn look a little less dreary. The parking lot had been newly plowed and scraped and it was dry in places. I found Charlie in the sitting room with the frilly curtains.

"How's it going?"

"About what you'd expect. A lot of very sick people here. It's actually very convenient, not far from Brookside

Cemetery." He didn't smile, but there was a glint of mischief in his eyes.

His attempt at a humorous take on the situation was reassuring. Again, he hadn't mentioned wanting to die.

"You won't have to stay here long. You know what you have to do to get out of here."

"Don't worry. I'll work on the walking."

I told him about Ross's offer to call the Maytag man who bought used appliances.

"Go ahead. I'll need the money. I'm sharing a room here to the tune of $500 a week. Verna called me. She wants to buy your aunt's desk and the spool bedroom set. I told her I wasn't selling the desk, but I'd sell her the bedroom set. She claims she's attached to it." His tone was disgusted.

"It's not surprising she's interested in the only antiques you own. The spool bedroom set is valuable or she wouldn't want it. I'll see if I can get it appraised."

"She said she'd give me $100 for it."

"I'll see what I can find out."

Later after leaving Angel Inn, I called Ross from the sports bar where I'd had coffee with Allen a couple of days before. "Charlie is willing to sell the appliances. Tomorrow we are removing his furniture, and if the Maytag dealer is interested in the appliances, he'll have to come for them Thursday morning. Do you happen to know an appraiser for antiques?"

"I do. But he's in Florida for the winter."

I sighed.

"That's too bad." It was a long-standing custom in the snow-clogged North Country for some residents to spend winters in Florida.

"There used to be several others, but now he's the only one. Wally has been working with antique dealers, probably from Syracuse; he'll know the value of the bed."

"I don't think Wally will be much help."

Ross gave me the phone number of the Maytag dealer. I arranged for the appliances to be picked up Thursday morning. Then I drove to Agnes's house where I told her about my day.

"Gosh, you have more ups and downs than Helen Trent," she said, then explained, "I listened to *The Romance of Helen Trent*, a soap opera, on the radio for years. It came on after lunch each day."

"My mom used to listen to it, too. And yes, there is a lot going on. I'm worn out with the whole business."

"You'll need to take a day off before you go home."

"That sounds like a good idea," I said wearily. As tired as I felt, I would probably toss and turn all night, dreading what lay ahead.

Chapter 23

Wednesday, February 16, 1994

I arrived at the Washington Street house before ten. The day was overcast with threatening dark clouds, and it had warmed to the low 30s. If the temperature continued to rise, the day might bring rain. I hoped it would hold off during the hours ahead when we would remove Charlie's things from the house.

Allen waited in front of the house with Paul and another young man. "This is Paul's brother Frank," he said. "He's come along to help."

Frank, like his brother, wore a sweatshirt and a down vest. But there the brothers' resemblance ended. Frank wore a folded blue bandana around his head to contain his curly brown hair. With long-eyelashes fringing blue eyes and regular features, he looked like a teenage heartthrob.

"Thanks for doing this," I said.

"I've told the fellas that they're to keep an eye on you. I'm not expecting any problems, but it doesn't hurt to take precautions," Allen said.

"You sound like my father," I said.

"That's right. Addison would do the same for my daughters."

Wally drove up in his van and got out. Verna was with him.

"Good morning," I said cheerfully. "We'll get all this done, and then we'll be out of your way."

Verna came to my side. "Charlie said he'd sell me the spool bedroom set for $100."

"He told me you had offered him $100, not that he'd accepted the offer."

"Charlie said he'd take a check. Here, I've written it out." She waved the check at me. Something about her gesture was threatening.

I almost laughed in her face. "I don't believe he said any such thing, but you are dealing with me, not him. If you want the bedroom set, and it must be worth more than $100 or you wouldn't want it, I'll take only cash. And if you can't come up with the cash, it will go on the truck with Charlie's other belongings." He had told me that all three-bedroom sets in the house belonged to him, but I doubted he would ever need them again.

"You have no right!" Verna spewed out the words as if they were acid.

"I have all the right in the world. I'm Charlie's power of attorney." I turned from her and walked over to where Allen was leaning on his pick-up truck.

"Let's get to work." He signaled to his helpers.

I unlocked the door and we went inside, followed by Wally. Verna stormed off in a huff.

I had a list of what belonged to my uncle. Under Wally's watchful gaze, I directed Allen's two helpers. "You can begin with the big TV."

The two men picked it up, carried it to Allen's truck, and returned. "There are two-bedroom sets in the front and back bedrooms upstairs," I said.

A few minutes later, Allen wrestled the heavy maple dresser from Charlie's room down the stairs by himself. He had removed the drawers, but it was still a heavy piece of furniture. I wanted to protest, yet I didn't know how I could do so without offending him.

Before long, the pickup truck was full. Allen came to where I stood in the hall. "We'll have to rent a Ryder truck and a bigger storage area. I'll take Paul with me to pick up a truck while you arrange a bigger storage area. Frank will follow you and begin unloading."

"I'm sorry," I said. "I had no idea Charlie had so much stuff."

"It's a challenge, not a problem," he said. "In a day or two, this will be all behind us."

After finishing at the storage rental office, it was the middle of the afternoon before I was back at the Washington Street house. Though the clouds were still dark, fortunately, there was no sign of rain. A Ryder truck with the tailgate open sat in the driveway.

Verna stood at the door with Wally, waiting for me.

"Here's your money." The bills were folded, and she all but threw them at me.

I put the bills in my pocket. "Correction. It's not my money, but money an old man needs to pay for his continuing care. I see no reason you have to get the bedroom set out of the house today since Wally should be in possession of the house by the weekend, and you can remove it at your leisure."

Verna glared at me.

Allen came down the stairs carrying two big boxes. He put them down and came to my side. "You can leave the spool bedroom set. I've sold it to Verna."

"That's fine with me," he said. "We've got enough stuff to fill the bigger storeroom. While you were out, the Maytag man called. He'll be here tomorrow at ten for the appliances."

A furious look passed over Verna's face. "You have no right to take the appliances!"

I refused to argue with her and turned to Allen as if Verna hadn't spoken.

Verna stepped in front of me, blocking my way. I coolly stepped around her.

"Allen, will we be able to finish this today?"

"It gets dark early, and we'll barely get everything in the storage area before the fellas have to get back for milking."

"You can't do this!" Verna shrieked.

158

I continued to ignore her. The memory of my father continuing to mow the lawn while an unwelcomed insurance salesman lay in wait to talk with him flashed through my mind.

I had no idea that Charlie had brought so much stuff with him to the marriage. "I'm sorry, it's taking so long."

Allen waved a hand dismissively. "We better get moving. Verna, it's time for you to leave. I'll follow you out." He picked up the boxes and inclined his head in the direction of the exit.

Verna muttered under her breath, hesitated for a moment, then grabbed her coat and headed for the door. Allen brought up the rear.

Wally came into the hallway from the living room. It was as if he had been loitering just inside the door to see what would happen.

"Wally," I said. "Charlie was particularly concerned that you give me his first wife's family silver."

"I know where it is. I'll get it." Wally retreated into the dining room. I stared after him, perplexed. He'd acquiesced readily to my request. Maybe he'd realized the futility of making a scene.

Frank came down the stairs with more boxes. These looked dusty, as if they had been under a bed or in the attic. The thought occurred to me that boxes from Charlie's house were moved here and had never been opened.

"That's about it," he said. "We'll be leaving for the storage area."

Wally emerged from the dining room with a silver box. He handed it to me. I passed it to Frank who was heading out with a last load for the truck.

"Thanks, Wally."

Allen came back into the house.

"We're going to lock up here."

I turned to Wally. "It's time for you to leave, too."

"I don't like being pushed out of my own house," Wally whined.

"The house will be yours soon enough," Allen said. "Right now, though, we're locking her down."

Wally slowly took his coat from the coat rack and put it on. "Did anyone ever tell you that you're butting in where you don't belong?" Wally asked him.

"More than once," Allen countered calmly. He shooed Wally out the front door. "I'm going over to the storeroom to help the fellas unload. Phyllis, you don't need to come along."

"I'll go by to see how Charlie is doing."

Everyone left the house, and in the fading light, Allen locked it.

At the truck, he motioned me aside. "We'll need to be here early tomorrow morning. The refrigerator needs cleaning out and there's lots of trash in the kitchen."

"I noticed that. You can't miss it. And I'm not surprised that Wally hasn't purchased any garbage bags for a while."

"Is nine too early?"

"Agnes is up every morning at seven. So I won't disturb her. By the way, she has suggested that when we get the job done here, we take a day off. What do you think?"

Allen brightened, and I noticed how tired he looked. "I'd like that. It's been a while since I've had a day off."

I went to Angel Inn and to fill Charlie in. I didn't stay long. I was as exhausted as if I had done the toting and carrying all by myself. The day had been jarring and uncomfortable, but everything had gone as planned. I feared there might be trouble with the appliances tomorrow. The Latin origin of the name *Verna* came from the word for spring. I half expected that she would "spring" something on us tomorrow. Verna *spring, spring*, how I missed my wordplay with Alex.

Chapter 24

Thursday, February 17, 1994

The lack of sleep I had been getting for many nights was taking its toll, and I was dragging when I arrived at the Washington Street house at nine. It was another frigid day, and Allen was sitting in his truck with the motor running. He got out when I arrived, and we went in together. The kitchen was a mess. Through the kitchen window, I saw Paul shoveling a path to the back door.

"The appliances will have to go out through the back," Allen explained. "And we'll have to pick up the trash so the men can have room to maneuver them out."

"Allen, you think of everything."

"I've brought garbage bags; we'd better get busy."

The wastebasket overflowed with beer cans. We picked those up first. Then I held the bag while he emptied the it. Under the sink was a stinky can of garbage. Allen emptied it into the garbage bag. I spotted several soiled diapers and almost gagged. The bag was full. I tied it off and put it by the door before opening another.

"I'm sure Charlie would want the refrigerated cleaned out before selling it. This still is a small town full of gossips." I heard Allen's knees creak as he squatted down in front of the refrigerator. It came as a shock to me because he seemed so strong, determined, and in charge, I had all but forgotten that he was Charlie's age. I hoped yesterday's move haven't been too much for him.

"Hold the garbage bag," he said as if he realized my thoughts were elsewhere.

I held the bag while he dumped partly used jars of mustard, salad dressing, and jam into the bag. He plucked wilted celery, sprouted potatoes, and half a head of cabbage, black with mold, from the vegetable drawer. The meat tray contained moldy cheese and an opened package of hot dogs. The new garbage bag was soon about half full. Allen stood, drained a half-gallon of orange juice and a large bottle of Coke that had gone flat into the sink, and then deposited the juice container and the Coke bottle in the garbage bag. He opened the freezer and tossed into the garbage bag unlabeled plastic containers of food, a half-used, opened package of frozen peas, and a pork chop, rusty with freezer burn.

"I wish we had time to give this a good cleaning," Allen said.

"The appliances are fairly new." I tied off the second garbage bag. "And the man buying them will be getting a bargain. So, I'm not going to worry about how clean they are.

I'll check the washer and dryer to make sure that no one has left anything in them."

Allen took the garbage bags outside, and I opened the washer. Nothing. I moved to the dryer and took out a pair of little-boy pants. I experienced a twinge. Was I really doing this, putting a mother down on her luck and her child out on the street? Probably one reason Verna wanted the bed was that she was planning on staying in the house. And staying in the house without appliances would be impossible.

I decided to look for Charlie's medications. I opened the cupboard nearest the sink, the obvious place for them. Nothing. I opened cupboards filled with dishes, glasses, and cups. No medicine. Paper napkins in a napkin holder, salt and pepper shakers, and a dirty coffee cup stood on the kitchen table next to a bottle of baby aspirin. If he had kept medicines on the kitchen table, there was no sign of them.

I was turning the mystery of the disappearance or lack of the medicines over in my mind and wiping off the stove when I heard the front door open. I put down my cloth and went to the front hallway. Verna, her stepfather Bill Landis, and a dark-haired woman I hadn't seen before were in the hallway. The woman, wearing a bulky nylon jacket, was in her fifties, overweight with a puffy, made-up face. She glared at me.

"What are you doing here?" I asked Verna. I'd so hoped that I was through with her.

Paul joined me in the hallway. He turned to the man. "Please move your truck. It's blocking the driveway, and we're expecting the Maytag people here any minute."

"No-o," Bill Landis said drawing out the word for emphasis.

My forehead felt like someone was tightening a metal band around it. This was the confrontation I had feared.

Paul moved a step closer to me, and I was glad for the presence of the sturdy dairy farmer.

"I'm Mabel Landis, Verna's mother and Miriam's daughter," the older woman said, narrowing her eyes. "We're here because you have no right to take the appliances from the house."

Verna's refusal to leave the house was beginning to make sense. Mabel was probably upset about the appliances because she had made some sort of deal about the house with Wally. Charlie stood in the way of their plans.

"You have no proof that the appliances belong to Charlie Hall," Bill Landis said.

"I don't need proof," I said with a calmness that belied my agitated state. "If Charlie says he bought all the appliances, that's enough for me. I've never known him to lie."

"You can't do this! Once the appliances came into the house, they became joint property." Mabel Landis's face had grown red. She clearly was trying to pick a fight with me, just as Verna had earlier.

"I'm not moving my truck." Landis pulled back his shoulders in a threatening stance.

I was becoming exasperated, and I wasn't sure how long I could maintain my calm outward demeanor. "All I'm trying to do is get together enough money for an 87-year-old man to be able to pay for his care."

"We want a bill of sale," Landis said.

I stood a little straighter and gave him a commanding stare, the kind of stare my father would have given in this situation. "I'll take full responsibility."

Allen came to join us. Feeling the tension in the room, he looked at me questioningly. "The Maytag men are here."

"Verna's stepfather is refusing to move his truck."

"We'll see about that. Where's the phone? I'm calling the police."

"In the living room," I said.

"Okay...okay," Landis said. "But you haven't heard the last of this." He turned and stamped out the front door.

"Wally won't stand for this," Mabel said. "You are violating Wally's rights."

"Wally isn't here," I said evenly, "because he knows full well that Charlie bought all the appliances, just as he did the TV."

"You can say what you want," Mabel said. "My husband is only moving his truck because we know the police will side with your uncle. The Troopers and the cops are thick as thieves. The fact is the appliances were given to my mother."

"I'm not discussing it any further" I turned away from the woman's hateful stare. "I've got work to do."

I retreated to the kitchen. Allen and Paul followed. I closed the door and leaned against it for a few seconds.

"Whew, that was pretty bad. Thanks, Paul, for standing by me in there."

He shook his head and smiled. "Think nothing of it."

Two burly appliance men appeared at the back door, and Paul helped the men remove the stove, refrigerator, washer, and dryer. When they finished, I signed a bill of sale.

"You can pick up your check later this morning at the store," the older man said.

Just then, Wally, wearing a disgruntled look, came into the kitchen with its gaping holes where the appliances had been. I was tempted to say something to him about getting his sister and her husband to do his dirty work, but I was too worn down to say anything beyond what was absolutely necessary.

"Now that we have everything out of the house, we'll have to get the gas and electric cut off so Charlie won't continue to be billed."

"You can't turn off the utilities this time of year," Wally protested. "Without heat, the pipes will freeze."

"I'm telling you about our plans so you can go to Niagara Mohawk Power tomorrow and arrange for them to be turned on in your name. You'll be able to sign the papers for the house and pick up the keys from your lawyer sometime in the afternoon."

Wally looked chagrined, beaten. "I guess that's it then."

"Yes, we'll get the cable box and lock up the house," I said. "We'll be out of here in ten minutes. Tomorrow it will be yours. Allen, will you please get the cable box while I secure the back door?"

With slumped shoulders, Wally followed Allen to the living room and then out the front door while I locked the house. I was too tired to feel elated at getting Charlie free from the claws of the vultures. And there was still the lawyer, the power company, the cable company, and the other utilities to deal with.

"Paul's taking my truck back to my place," Allen said. "I suspect you could use a cup of coffee."

"I'd like nothing better," I said.

Later, at the little restaurant we'd visited before, the owner brought us two fragrant cups of fresh coffee. I took a sip, savoring the simple pleasure of good coffee. "Do you think they'll make good on any of their threats?"

"I don't think so. If they had a leg to stand on, they wouldn't have to resort to bullying."

"Will they go to Wally's lawyer over the appliances?"

"Probably. But the lawyer, no doubt, will tell them there is nothing he can do."

"It seems a lot of fuss over $475 worth of appliances."

"I suspected all along they thought Charlie had deep pockets, probably because he has a state pension. He may have unintentionally led them to think he had more resources than he does."

I shook my head. "I imagine, on one hand, he was proud to be able to support Miriam, and on the other, he must have become increasingly aware that her family was taking advantage of him. And none of them have stepped up to help him."

"Maybe the ones that are decent just washed their hands of the whole deal after Wally cheated them out of what they felt was their inheritance."

"Miriam's daughter Jill said those very words. It all comes down to money."

"Greed."

"Speaking of money, I want to pay for the Ryder truck. And I'd like to do something for Paul and Frank."

"The truck is taken care of. We didn't even have it for 24 hours. Maybe when you get home, you could send me a couple those sweatshirts with hoods from Virginia. Paul and Frank would get a kick out of that."

"Of course. It doesn't seem like much. I certainly appreciated all they did."

"Don't worry. They know I'll take care of them like I always do."

In spite of Miriam's antiques and pretensions, Allen, with no pretensions at all, was a man with power and wealth. "Thanks, Allen."

"What's next?"

"After I pick up the appliance check, I'm going to walk with Charlie at the nursing home. My plan is to arrange a walking test at United Helpers on Saturday in Ogdensburg."

"I better go with you," Allen said.

"I guess it wouldn't hurt. If he passes the test, maybe we can arrange to move him in there early in the week. And once he's there, maybe I can go home." I didn't realize how heartfelt the words sounded.

An empathetic look passed over Allen's face. "Your family must be missing you. I know I will."

I smiled. "I can imagine it will be good to get your life back."

"This is the most fun I've had in years." He took out a $5 bill and left it on the table. He must have felt powerless when he could nothing about his wife's dementia. Helping us had been something he could do.

I gave him a questioning look as we stood to leave. "When does the fun begin?"

He laughed. "Time for us to get on with it."

That night in bed, I tossed and turned, still upset by the events of the day. I was cold, and couldn't seem to get warm even under Agnes's heavy wool blankets. I was uneasy about stripping the house of the appliances. I kept seeing the little boy's pants in the dryer. Yet, Miriam's family had been living off Charlie, and it was time to bring that to an end. I wondered if Wally—who probably owed both the gas and electric companies—could get the utilities turned on. Leaving a house empty in February with no heat would no doubt lead to other problems, burst pipes, or worse.

I wondered again if Verna or Wally hadn't done something to try to hasten Charlie's death. I regretted not questioning him about his medications and diet prior to his admission to the hospital. At the most appropriate time to do so, I was convinced he was dying. I'd have to trust Charlie's well-honed State Police instincts and my own. He'd been adamant that he couldn't return to the Washington Street house. And I agreed.

A plow went by and I saw the clock in the light of the headlights. It was almost five o'clock, and I hadn't slept. I closed my eyes and tried to focus on what had to be done in the coming day.

Chapter 25

Friday, February 18, 1994

The next morning, Agnes gave me a hot breakfast of oatmeal with maple syrup. Fortified with this hearty fare, I brushed two inches of powdery snow from the Oldsmobile's windshield. It was ten degrees, and high diaphanous clouds obscured the weak sun. I was eager to get the day over with. I felt like a weary marathon runner who sees the end in sight and needs to muster one last push to get to the finish line.

In Watertown, I picked Allen up at his house. He directed me to the Niagara Mohawk Power office east of the city. Inside, I explained that I needed the power and gas turned off at my uncle's house.

"I can send someone out to read the meters today," the clerk said. "And the man can turn off the gas. To have it turned on in someone else's name, they will have to come by the office. Who will be taking over the house?"

"Wally Thompson," I said.

The clerk's face registered dismay. It was clear that she had dealings with Wally in the past. "I'll send somebody over there right away."

"That will be fine," Allen said. "We'll meet your man there."

Outside in the car, I asked. "Do we really need to go by the house again?"

"Probably not, I just want to make sure the meter reader doesn't have any problems."

We drove to the Washington Street house and waited in the car. Fortunately, neither Verna nor Wally showed up. When the meter reader left, I turned to Allen.

"Is the cable place next?"

"Yes. And we better get a receipt from the cable people when we turn the cable box in."

"Definitely."

Returning the cable box was no problem. It was noon by the time we were done.

"Let's have lunch," Allen suggested.

The little restaurant where we'd had coffee smelled of French fries and hamburgers. I ordered an egg-salad sandwich and he ordered a piece of chocolate pie. All along, I noticed Allen had eaten little or nothing when we had shared a meal.

"We're almost done," I said.

"We've got to get the water turned off. Maybe we can just give them a call. I don't think we'll need a power of attorney."

I found a phone book and called the office from the payphone in the restaurant to explain that I wanted the water turned off. The clerk asked me to hold for a minute while she checked the records. Moments later, she said. "The water is in Miriam Thompson's name."

"That's fine. We won't need to turn it off then."

I told Allen what I had learned.

"We'll go by the post office and do a change of address for Charlie," he said. "And then we can turn the keys into the lawyer and you can sign whatever is necessary."

I took a deep breath. The list of things still to do was endless.

Twenty minutes later, we were in the old Woolworth Building. We rode in a creaking elevator smelling of stale tobacco smoke to the fourth floor. I wasn't looking forward to meeting the lawyer I'd put on the carpet years ago about my aunt's estate.

The heavy oak door to his office looked like it was from a stage set for an old movie. I half expected the lawyer would look like an aged Humphrey Bogart.

A plump, gray-haired woman, wearing glasses, the frames studded with rhinestones, sat at a desk in an outer office.

"May I help you?" she asked.

"I'm Phyllis Haislip and this is Charles Hall's friend, Allen Hodge. We're here to see Oliver Wisner."

"He's expecting you," the secretary said. "When I first heard your name, I wondered if you were related to the Mary Haislip I went to school with."

"I'm sorry. I don't know Mary Haislip," I said. I was apprehensive about the coming meeting and not eager today to play the *who do you know that I know*-game with the secretary.

"Let me see," the secretary said, undeterred. "Mary was the only Haislip I knew, but I've known plenty of Hodges."

"And they're probably related to me," Allen said politely. "I have two daughters and they both graduated from Watertown High."

"What were their names?"

I had to admire him for playing the game when all I wanted to do was shout at her to hurry up.

"The eldest is Susanne and my youngest is Elizabeth. Liz, everyone calls her."

"Did they once have a green convertible with a white roof?"

"That's them," he said. "And I still have the car. It is one pretty car and in good shape for its age."

The woman brightened now that the connection has been made. She stood. "I'll tell Mr. Wisner that you're here."

A moment later, she ushered us into a big room that smelled of pipe tobacco. The walls were lined with bookshelves holding ponderous legal tomes. A frail old man rose from a big walnut desk to greet us.

I was not surprised that Oliver Wisner was old, but I was surprised that he was so stooped and wizened. I couldn't help but feel a bit sorry that I had to resort to the New York State Bar Association to get my aunt's will settled. Even 15 years ago, when he'd been about 65, the law, outside of the usual transactions, must have been a stretch for his abilities. It flashed through my mind that Charlie's problems with the lawyer and with Verna and Wally may have occurred because my uncle wasn't very good at standing up for himself. Dad, in contrast, would have fired the dilatory lawyer and refused to put with the shenanigans of Verna and Wally.

I saw papers on the lawyer's desk.

"I gather you have drawn up the legal papers for turning over the house," I said.

Mr. Wisner smiled, revealing yellowed teeth and receding gums. "All set for you to sign here. And Mr. Hodge can witness it." He passed the papers to me along with a pen from a fancy pen stand.

I signed in the designated places, and then Allen carefully signed his name. He returned the papers to the lawyer. I reached into my pocket for the house keys and put them on top of the papers.

Allen stood, and I got to my feet too. We shook hands again and left the office. I felt lighter, freer than I had been since arriving in Watertown. The whole transaction had taken less than five minutes. We walked to the elevator.

"I'm relieved it all went smoothly," I said.

Allen chuckled. "I called him yesterday to urge him on a bit, but he looks none the worse for it."

"Allen, good men are hard to find. How did I ever find you?"

"Just lucky, I guess."

From the lawyer's office, we went directly to Angel Inn to tell Charlie the news.

"It's over," I said when we found him in the common room. "You are no longer legally responsible for the Washington Street house."

Charlie's face lit up and he raised both hands in a gesture of exultation. The years seemed to slip away, and for a few moments he looked like a little boy who received a much-coveted fire engine for Christmas.

"Thank you. I'm so glad to be out from under the burden of that house."

"If I can arrange it, would you be up for a trip to Ogdensburg tomorrow to take the walking test?" I asked.

"My walking got better five minutes ago now that I'm no longer carrying around that house." He was still grinning.

"Okay," I said. "I'll set it up."

I delivered Allen back to his house. "Allen, I'll pick you up at nine."

Heading to Carthage, I drove through the darkening countryside. Bright yellow squares of light pierced the gloom in barns along the way as farmers set about the evening milking. Overhead, a full moon rose, casting blue shadows on the fields of snow.

I pondered again how Charlie might have been caught up in such a mess. I remembered Dad's impatience with both his mother and his brother. They were gentle, kindhearted, easygoing, and prone to go along with the flow. Years ago, the State Troopers had recognized Charlie's mild, milquetoast manner when they had him pose as a soap salesman during prohibition. He was very successful in ferreting out speakeasies. What the Troopers must have recognized, and what I had always known, was that under his gentle demeanor was a core of integrity and strength. Circumstances and the years had taken their toll, and almost destroyed him, but he was stronger than the greedy relatives.

Charlie had been a Trooper for 41 years, something almost unheard of in the annals of the State Police. He hadn't risen in the ranks because that would have entailed removing his wife and invalid daughter from their beloved home. During the same years, Dad had advanced to become a sergeant and then a plain-clothed investigator, the state equivalent of the FBI.

Being the older brother, Dad on occasion had to get his brother out of the unintended consequences of his actions. Now all these years later, I was doing the same thing. And yet, in his defense, Charlie had been part of Miriam's family for 13 years. Anyone who has been part of an extended family knows that implies connections, responsibilities, and complications that someone outside the family can't truly appreciate. In the end, his kind, generous heart had landed him in a place he didn't want to be.

Chapter 26

Saturday, February 19, 1994

Saturday dawned bright and clear. The temperature was forecast to get above freezing, and I was grateful for a mild day for the Ogdensburg trip. I picked up Allen and we went on to Angel Inn where Charlie was waiting for us in the sitting room, frowning. "We have a problem," he said. "I can't get my shoes on."

I glanced down at his swollen ankles. Not another roadblock. Not now. I repeated Allen's words.

"It's not a problem, it's a challenge. What size shoes do you wear? I recall seeing a Walmart somewhere. We'll get you a new pair of shoes in the next biggest size."

He looked relieved. "Size nine and a half."

"You can wear your slippers to the car, and we'll pick up new shoes for you on the way out of town."

"Great. I don't want to *slip up* on the walking test," he said with a twinkle in his eye. "There's one other thing. "My Timex has stopped. Could you also get me a new battery for it?"

"I'll be glad to," I said, laughing. "It probably won't take much *time.*" It had never occurred to me until this moment that my son, Alex, might have gotten his love of wordplay from Charlie, and I loved making the connection.

"Allen, I'll drive up as close as I can to the door. I'd appreciate it if you'd walk out with Charlie."

"Sure enough," Allen said.

It took ten minutes to get Charlie into the car and his walker stowed in the trunk.

"Now I know how a man feels getting out of prison," he said as I drove away. "Whatever happens today, it's great to get out for a few hours."

At Walmart, I bought Charlie gray jogging shoes with Velcro closures in size ten and a half and had a battery installed in his Timex.

"We need to try on the shoes here in the parking lot," I said. "And here's your watch."

"Thank you. My *time* had run out, and you've given more *time,*" he said with a smile. When the shoes were on, Charlie stretched out his feet and laughed. "Now I know why the young people all wear these. They're light and comfortable. It's great to have shoes on again."

"Speaking of time," Allen said, "We'd best be going."

We were soon zooming in the direction of Ogdensburg.

"Allen, do you have grandchildren?" I asked.

"I sure do," he replied conversationally. "Maryanne's daughter is adopted, and Liz has two daughters and one son. I don't see them much. They live near New York City. But my youngest granddaughter is something else. Last summer, she worked for a moving company."

"In the office?" I asked.

"Nope, as a mover." He paused.

"Is she big and strong?"

"She's about five foot five and probably doesn't weigh 100 pounds."

"How'd she happen to do that kind of heavy work?" Charlie asked.

"She's a pistol. Always up to something!"

"Sounds like her grandfather," I said.

"Maybe that's why I'm so fond of her," Allen offered. "I don't know about her brother. He's a standup comic, or so he says."

I could tell from Allen's tone that being a comedian didn't fit into his practical worldview.

"He apparently has some success performing in New York City clubs."

We fell into silence. I hoped Allen wasn't too hard on his grandson who wasn't following a traditional career path.

We exited the Interstate and passed through small towns and by farms. In one farmyard, children were building a snowman. At another place, little kids were sliding. The countryside looked like something on a Christmas card. Charlie took it in like a thirsty man enjoying a drink of cold water on a hot day.

Next, we came to the place where the road followed the St. Lawrence River, giving us a view of an expanse of sky.

"Those clouds are looking *serious*," Charlie said.

It took me a minute to get it. *Cirrus.* I laughed in delight.

"Charlie, Alex would call that 'a groaner.'"

Charlie's wordplay was reassuring. He was in fine spirits, and that couldn't help but improve his chances of walking the required distance.

It was a little after eleven when I pulled up in front of the assisted-living facility. Allen and Charlie made their way to the front door while I parked the car. They were sitting in the lobby when I joined them.

"What do you think, Charlie? Is this a place you would like to live?" I asked.

He looked around at the fieldstone fireplace, the tasteful furnishings, and the bright lobby.

"I'll take it if we can get it," he said with enthusiasm.

A staff member had apparently notified Mrs. Warren, and she came to greet us. I introduced my uncle and Allen.

"Mr. Hall, I've told your niece this, but when I checked with our nursing home, several of the nurses gave you glowing recommendations. They told me how often you visited your daughter."

Charlie blushed. "The nurses are very nice."

"We have a waiting list for places here, but we have a policy that priority is always given to family members. So, that puts you at the head of the list. However, if you're not able to move in this coming week, the place will have to go to the next person."

"Tell me what I have to do."

"Our guidelines say you have to be able to walk 40 feet."

"Can I use my walker?"

"Of course."

A smile crept onto Charlie's face. "I can do that."

"Mrs. Haislip and Mr. Hodge, if you will wait here, I'll accompany Mr. Hall down the corridor."

Charlie struggled to his feet, and I was suddenly afraid he wouldn't be able to do it. He struggled for balance for a moment, then pushed the walker forward, putting one foot in front of the other.

"How do you like my shoes?" he asked Mrs. Warren as they moved away. "They're jogging shoes, and pretty soon I'll be jogging."

"I hope so," Mrs. Warren said.

I crossed my fingers as they walked to the corridor and disappeared down it. It seemed like a long time, but it was probably less than ten minutes until they returned.

Charlie smiled broadly. "Did I pass?"

"Mr. Hall, you've passed with flying colors," Mrs. Warren announced. "Now, if you come with me, I'll show you the available room. It's on the second floor, but it's near the elevator."

I sagged in relief as they disappeared in the direction of the elevator. I felt a bit like I did when I left Alex for his first day at kindergarten. Like my five-year-old, Charlie seemed propelled by enthusiasm to explore his new world.

When they returned, Charlie gave us a thumbs-up as he accompanied Mrs. Warren into her office. I had done so much in his name in the last weeks that it was a relief that he would be signing the necessary papers.

In the car again for the return trip to Watertown, I asked, "Charlie, do you want to visit Charlene?"

He gave me a guilty look. "It's been too long since I've seen her, but I'm really exhausted. And within days I'll be her next-door neighbor, and I can see her regularly. Or so Mrs. Warren told me."

"When did Mrs. Warren say you could move in?" Allen asked.

"Next Tuesday or Wednesday."

"I've been thinking," Allen said. "Charlie, you've got a whole lot of stuff in that storage area. Maybe on Monday, if you are up to it, you can go through it and determine what you'll need in your new place."

I looked at my watch. It was going on one o'clock, and we hadn't eaten lunch.

"Charlie, Allen, do you want to stop for something to eat?" I asked.

"Maybe we can stop at one of those drive-through places," Allen offered

"That would be perfect," Charlie said.

Later, back at the nursing home, I told Charlie that I was taking tomorrow off. "Try to get some rest. We're going to have a couple of busy days next week."

After leaving, I dropped Allen at his house. "We've been invited to Agnes's daughter's house on Lake Bonaparte tomorrow," I said. "Do you still want to join us for a day out?"

"I wouldn't miss it."

"I'll go to church with Agnes in the morning. Could you come to her house about one?"

"I'm looking forward to it. And to meeting Agnes. We've talked so much on the phone; I feel I already know her."

Clouds obscured the late afternoon sun as I drove toward Carthage. Charlie had had two good days in a row. He liked the facility in Ogdensburg as much as I did, and he passed the walking test. Through the trauma of the last weeks, Agnes had been supportive, even though I had little time to spend with her. I was glad that she made the suggestion that we take a day off and had planned something for us to do. World-weariness – and something that almost passed for contentment – settled over me like a heavy blanket. I yawned. Maybe tonight I'd finally get a good night's sleep.

Chapter 27

Sunday, February 20, 1994

The next morning, I called Charlie. "Hello," he said. His voice was thick as if he hadn't used it much this morning.

"I'm just checking in. How are you doing?"

"I'm doing good. I got a good sleep last night."

"So did I."

"Agnes has invited me to go to church with her, and this afternoon we'll go to see her daughter's new home on Lake Bonaparte."

"You've got a full day. I'll see you tomorrow," he said.

The day was sunny, and I saw on Agnes's porch thermometer as we headed out that it was 25 degrees. We walked the half-mile to the redbrick church on sidewalks that were mostly clear, with the icy patches heavily sanded.

I hadn't been to Saint James Church, where I'd attended as a child, for 30 or more years. Inside, the familiar smells of incense and wet boots greeted me. The church was smaller than I remembered and prettier. It didn't appear to have changed at all, except there was now a new altar in front of the original one. In the 1960s, the altars in Catholic churches were modified so that the priest didn't spend the whole mass with his back to the congregation. The main altar was painted white, and the new altar was made of white marble. On both sides were huge paintings of saints, their robes rendered in rich, warm hues of melon, gold, green and blue. The paintings were emotional, but also beautiful. I was immediately brought back to my childhood to a more magical time in my life where the saints and angels along with Santa and the Easter Bunny were mysteries that only adults understood.

We found seats in one of the hard, oak pews, not far from where I used to sit with my mother.

The music began, and I whispered to Agnes, "Nothing has changed. The music is still as bad as I remember it."

Agnes smiled. "You'll find the sermon pretty much the same too."

When it came time for the sermon, I tried without success to focus on the priest's words. My gaze became fixed on the filigreed sanctuary lamp. It was ornate, yet tasteful. In Evelyn Waugh's *Brideshead Revisited*, the sanctuary lamp had stood for the triumph of Catholicism after the loss of faith and sinfulness. But for me, it stood for the continuance of the life of the spirit amid all the changes of the years, and all the trials and pains of daily life.

The familiar words of the mass flowed over me like a Greek chorus. My reverie ended only when the altar boy chimed the cluster of altar bells to signal that the most sacred part of the mass was approaching. I didn't join the others receiving the sacrament. I had not been a communicant for years. But I closed my eyes, soaking in the peacefulness of the timeless ritual. Like much else in the last weeks, time seemed to bend back on itself, completing a circle.

After mass, Agnes chatted with several members of the congregation. I supplied the answers to their unasked questions by telling everyone that I was her dear friend's daughter. The mundane chitchat brought me back to the present as the after-church conversation turned into another version of *who do you know that I know?* I suppressed the smile that rose to my lips, then let it out. It felt good to want to grin again. After the stress of the last days, I was feeling much better. The worst was probably over for Charlie, and I was hopeful I would soon be able to return home.

At one o'clock, Allen arrived in his truck and parked in front of Agnes's house. He wore his Sunday tie and had shaved. I met him at the door.

"I see you had no trouble finding the house. Come on in."

"Your directions were spot-on and when I saw your uncle's car, I knew this was the right place."

Agnes came into the living room, and I introduced her to Allen.

"Thanks for taking care of our girl," he said.

"Why, you're the one who has made everything possible. I'm happy to finally meet you. Phyl can't say enough good things about you."

187

Allen shook his head as if the praise sat uneasily on him. "She's done right well herself."

"My daughter has just recently moved to Lake Bonaparte, and she has invited us to come by and see her place," Agnes explained.

"That sounds swell," he said. "I haven't been to Lake Bonaparte in, let's see maybe sixty years. After that, if we have time, there's someplace I'd like to show you."

"That sounds intriguing," Agnes said with a smile.

The roads were bare as I drove the fifteen miles to the side road that led to Agnes's daughter's house. The lake had once belonged to Joseph Bonaparte, Napoleon's brother, who owned a lot of land in the area. Agnes gave directions as the paved road gave way to gravel. It seemed to me if there were a map of the area, we had gone off it.

The house, a converted camp, sat right on the shore. Agnes's daughter, Sharlene and her husband Dick came out to greet us and gave us a tour of the lake house. I imagined that Allen was impressed, as I was, not only with the lovely setting, but also with the fact that everything in it was in its proper place.

In the garage, Sharlene showed us wood-burning equipment that she used to burn designs into wood and presented each of us a wooden magnet with an engraved map of the lake on it. It was as if the little magnet, and the place itself connected me with another part of my past life. When I was eleven years old, we moved from West Carthage to Star Lake in the Adirondack Park. There I swam in the crystalline lake, tromped through woods, skied down mountains, and learned to appreciate the backwoods lore of the Adirondacks.

"This is my very first magnet," Allen said. "It will remind me of today every time I open my refrigerator."

Back inside the house, Sharlene and Allen shared a beer, and Agnes and I had a piece of homemade cherry pie and freshly brewed coffee. We looked out of large windows at the stark beauty of the frozen lake. The woodstove fire crackled, and birds visited three feeders in the yard. We talked about old days in the Adirondacks, the big estates hidden away back in the woods, and the buck Dick killed last hunting season.

A pleasant hour and a half passed before I stood. "I hate to call a halt to this delightful visit, but Allen wants to show us something. So, we better move along. Thank you for your hospitality."

When we were in the car, I asked. "Where to, Allen?"

"I'd like to show you and Agnes my farm in Croghan."

"Great. It's been years since I've been to Croghan," I said.

Agnes chimed in. "I'm always up for a little drive in the countryside."

Croghan was a tiny village about a thirty-minute drive from Carthage. It had been famous for years for Croghan baloney, a particularly delicious local sausage, and also for maple syrup.

Within the hour, we were on an isolated dirt road not far out of town. "The farm is up on the right," Allen said. "Turn in just beyond that big maple. No one lives there now. But it was my wife's family homestead."

I hadn't heard the word *homestead* in ages, and it brought to mind the settlement of the American West.

The driveway to the house and barn was plowed, and the property looked well cared for.

"I'll give you a tour," he said. "Starting with the barn."

Agnes and I stepped into the still dim interior. The cold barn smelled faintly of old hay and automotive oil. It was filled with vintage vehicles: a 1936 oil truck with a faded Esso sign painted on the side, an ancient flat-bed logging truck from around 1945, a 1940s-era Ford, and a 1950s Studebaker. Along one wall was an assortment of farm equipment, including an early combine harvester.

"Wow," I said. "Where did you get all this?"

"The vehicles were all mine at one time or another," he said. "The equipment came with the farm."

It had long been popular in this area for folks to keep every vehicle they had ever owned. On back roads it wasn't unusual to see rusted hulks in yards. Allen was obviously well steeped in that tradition.

"I've got a model A in my barn in Watertown," Allen continued proudly. "And my girls' convertible."

We walked from the barn to the house. He unlocked the padlock in moments. "How do you remember all the combinations?" I asked.

"It's easy. They're all the last four numbers of my phone number."

I might have known it. Allen had everything in his world organized.

Inside, the house smelled closed up and musty. To my eyes, everything in it was right out of a movie set about farm life in the early part of the twentieth century. The original furniture was still in place, including an uncomfortable-looking horsehair sofa. There was a shelf made of the wooden spools that once were used for thread. Walking around the house gave me the unsettling feeling that I was trespassing in someone's home.

In the kitchen, there was an impressive, green kitchen range standing on legs. From pictures, I knew they were usually the center of the house because they were used for cooking, heat, and hot water. I stood for a moment admiring it, trying to figure out what the various compartments were for.

"There's a story about that stove," Allen said. "One day when I was courting my wife and she'd gone to town with her family, Carlton and I took the feet off the stove. When they got home, the stove was sitting on the floor." I was hard to imagine Allen's brother who had been so unhappy at Whispering Pines taking part in this prank.

"I can imagine that made you popular with Esther's family."

"Once they'd seen it and we'd had our fun, we put them right back on. And in the years that followed, Esther's father liked to tell everyone the story."

Allen's reminiscences made the empty house come alive, and the earlier uneasy feeling that I was trespassing disappeared. The people who had lived here were just out, and they'd return and find nothing disturbed.

He led us down to the cellar where a vegetable bin was full of apples. The smell brought back memories of my childhood, when we kept cabbages, potatoes, and apples in our cellar.

He took plastic bags from his pocket. "I wanted you both to have some apples."

It was late afternoon when we headed back to Carthage. I offered to take Allen and Agnes out to dinner.

"It's been a delightful afternoon, but there are some things I need to see to," Allen demurred.

Later, as I drove Agnes to a nearby restaurant, she commented, "What a lovely man!" Such a gentleman."

"Yes, he's very special." I realized how fond I'd become of Allen in just a few days. It was as if we'd been through a war together, and our shared struggle had forged a bond. "Today's been great. Thanks for encouraging us to take a day off."

Chapter 28

Monday, February 21, 1994

After the nice day out on Sunday, Monday turned cold and bleak again. I picked up Charlie at the nursing home and took him to the storage area. Allen was already there with the door open when we arrived. Paul was with him.

"I've brought him along to tussle some of the boxes," Allen said.

"Nice to meet you, Paul," Charlie said. "I understand you've been a big help." He looked around the crowded storage area. "I didn't realize I had so much stuff."

"Well, you do," Allen said, "and the plan today is to find what you need for the place in Ogdensburg, and get rid of stuff you don't. I've had Paul here free up a couple of chairs, but I'm thinking it's too cold to work outside."

"What will we do?" I asked, guessing Allen already had a plan.

"Let's set you up in my living room. Paul and I will bring stuff to you." The storage area was about two or three miles from the house, and I didn't envy Allen and Paul all the trips back and forth.

"That sounds good," Charlie said.

"Okay then. I'll meet you at the house."

At the house, Allen set up chairs for us in the middle of his living room and placed several boxes in front of each of us, along with trash bags for what we wanted to discard.

Allen disappeared with Paul, and Charlie and I began going through the first boxes. They were full of papers: ancient tax forms, canceled checks, advertisements. The next boxes were the same. It all had to be looked through, even though most of the stuff just went into garbage bags. Allen and Paul brought in bags of clothes: summer shirts, long underwear, Trooper socks, sweaters, hats, scarves, pajamas, and on and on.

We worked for three hours. At lunchtime, Allen brought us ham and cheese sandwiches and soda pop. He sat with us while we took a break to eat, but ate nothing. Where did he get his energy? It certainly wasn't from what he ate.

"How much more do we have to go through?" Charlie yawned.

"A lot," Allen said. "Do you want to quit for today and do some more tomorrow?"

"I'd like to move into United Helpers tomorrow," Charlie said. He perked up with effort. "And I'm sure Phyl is eager to get home."

"Okay," Allen said. "We'll just keep it coming."

Paul brought us two sealed boxes that were labeled Christmas decorations.

Charlie sighed deeply. "I'm not going to open these. Seeing decorations again from my Christmases with Ellen and Charlene will just make me sad. They can go in the trash."

One of the boxes Allen brought in was a box of photographs. "Certainly, you'll want to keep these," I said.

He sat back in his chair. "I want to show you something. Pass me the box." He rummaged through it for a few minutes before pulling out a photograph. "That's me and Eleanor Roosevelt. When she visited Lake Placid, she insisted that the Troopers who guarded her were good-looking. So, I was chosen for that special detail."

I studied the photograph for a moment. Charlie was sitting outside and beside him on a bench was Eleanor Roosevelt. He was indeed handsome.

"The First Lady was in residence for a month in the Adirondacks in 1933. And in addition to caring for my horse, I stuffed envelopes for her. She was diligent about answering her correspondence.

I studied the photograph again. "This is great. I never knew you had this. Dad told me you were a lady's man and dated the debutants that vacationed in the Adirondacks, but I don't recall him telling me you were detailed to Mrs. Roosevelt."

Charlie extracted another photo of him in the heavy sheepskin coat worn by Troopers in the open cars they drove. "And during the 1932 Olympics, I met Sonja Henie and dated a skater from Austria." He handed me an autographed photograph of several Olympic skaters, then took out a fragile, yellowed newspaper clipping. "I'm not mentioned in this article, but the most important thing I ever did was to testify in a school bus accident case when I was stationed in Clintonville in 1930. My testimony was crucial. The upshot of the whole thing was that the state education department led the country in mandating flashing lights and requiring traffic to stop for school buses.

"Well done!" It struck me that often seemingly ordinary lives were extraordinary.

He took a photo of a young man in a World War I uniform from the box. "This is your uncle, Walter. He went to Mexico with the army in 1916 and later was with the American Expeditionary Force in France. He was a balloonist, and after the war, he took part in a Harvard study of soldiers who had been gassed in France. I don't know what the war did to him, but he became a Spiritualist. He went to séances and all that kind of thing. In his spare time, he made and played violins. He died in 1933."

I shook my head. With regret, I realized that even though I had spent my life studying history, I knew little of my own family's history.

Charlie put the photograph back. "This whole box can go to Ogdensburg with me."

We got back to work. My writer's mind was still full of the rich stories he had told me. I realized I only saw people's lives as ordinary because I didn't know them. Every life was a story, and perhaps that's why we read stories, to glimpse another's life.

The afternoon wore on, and both Charlie and I grew more impatient with the task before us. We became a lot less discriminating with the debris from his life, and began throwing away things we barely looked at.

Through the haze of this soul-crushing process, I spotted an old letter. I studied it for a moment. "Look, what I've found. It's dated 1865. It's a Civil War letter."

Charlie shook his head. "Yes, I've already thrown away a bunch of them."

My heart fell. I hurriedly rescued a few other Civil War letters feeling bad that so many had already been thrown away. I was writing a children's Civil War novel, and eyewitness documents were being thrown away. Maybe the letters weren't of special value to Charlie, but having them in hand brought the past closer for me. Not to mention that they might help me with my research. The letters had survived for over a hundred years. It didn't feel right that they were being jettisoned like encumbering cargo at the end of a life. Charlie didn't seem to know about anything about the letters. He suspected they came from someone in his first wife's family.

Moving on, I rescued a packet of letters written by my aunt to her family from Long Island where she had her first teaching job. There wasn't time to read, but I couldn't resist dipping into them briefly. I'd never known my aunt as a young woman, but she was present in the letters. In one place she sketched a dress she had bought. Writing, even when not the wisdom of Seneca or the poignancy of Yeats, was more than words on paper. Writing outlasted death, and here was proof.

By four o'clock, we had assembled the necessary clothes for Charlie to take to Ogdensburg and eliminated most of the content of desks, dressers, and a chest. He was slumped in his chair and my back ached from extracting things from boxes and giving them to him to evaluate.

"I think we're done," Allen said. He pulled up a chair and seemed grateful to sit if only for a few minutes.

Charlie and I gave exhausted cheers. "How can we ever thank you?" I asked.

Allen gestured at the filled trash bags. "It had to be done. All that is left in the storage area is furniture."

"It has really turned me against *stuff*," I said. "At some point, your treasures become a burden. The only things of real value are family and friends."

"Emptying out one of the dressers, I found this coin," Allen said. He produced a copper penny dated 1754. "I'll clean it up and with your permission, Charlie, Phyllis can take it home with her. I've seen that she likes all things historical."

"It'll be a good souvenir of our day," Charlie said.

I looked at them both and shook my head. "I don't think you have to worry about me forgetting today. Or any of this."

That evening I told Agnes about my the ordeal. "If you want to do your family a favor, sell or give away stuff you don't want and will never use."

"As I've gotten into my later years, I've been thinking about that, but I've yet to do it." She grimaced. "I'm going to take that on as a project."

"If you do have anything of value, like letters, be sure to designate them as important," I warned her. "Otherwise, they'll get tossed along with old catalogs."

"I never keep catalogs," Agnes assured me.

"Ha! I wish I could say the same for Charlie."

"You look pretty spent."

"It was an exhausting day."

"Tomorrow will be better," she said with her characteristic optimism.

"Agnes, you've been a great help in the last difficult days."

"I wish I could have done more."

"You've given me shelter in the storm. You can't imagine how that's helped. Tonight, I'm going to change my airplane reservations, hopefully for the last time. I should be out of your hair on Wednesday."

"I've enjoyed having you here. February can be a dreary month."

"I don't know how much my mom understands now about what is happening. But from what Otis has said, she knows I've been staying with you, her friend of many years, and that has been a comfort to her."

"Your mom and I were good friends and spending time with you is almost as good as spending time with her. I wish I could do more for her, wished she wasn't so far away. Helping you out is the least I could do.

"Thanks, Agnes. Before I make my calls, could we please check the weather?"

Agnes turned on The Weather Channel with her remote. It wasn't time for the local report, but the national weather map showed a nor'easter barreling up the East Coast.

I studied the proposed trajectory of the storm and winced. "It doesn't look good for tomorrow." And when the local came on, the prediction was for six to 12 inches of snow beginning tomorrow night.

"The Weather Channel isn't always right," Agnes objected.

Before I could make my calls, the phone rang.

"It's for you," Agnes said. "Your uncle's neighbor."

I took the phone. "Hello, Ross."

"I visited Charlie today. He told me that you're transferring him to Ogdensburg tomorrow. Well done, Phyllis. It's just as well to get him away from Miriam's family."

"That wasn't necessarily my intention. But I see the advantages."

"I finally got in touch with someone I know and found out about Verna Loatwell.

"Allen calls her *that woman*."

"Well, it seems she's in a custody battle over the child with his father. They weren't married, but he accepted paternal rights at the time of the boy's birth. It's complicated, but I gather that it was okay for her to take the boy out of state, but unlawful for her to conceal him."

I took in this new information. "Verna probably cooked up some half-baked scheme with Wally to stay in his house indefinitely, keeping the boy's whereabouts from his father."

"That would be my guess."

"When we sold off the appliances, that was no longer an option."

"I suspect *that woman* and Wally thought that if your uncle died, they'd have the house just as it was."

"And they probably would have if I hadn't arrived. You've been a good friend to Charlie, Ross."

"He's an easy man to like."

"I hope to finally head home on Wednesday, if I'm not snowed in," I told him. "I've been away too long."

"I'll be in and out of Ogdensburg for my work, and I'll be sure to drop by and see Charlie. Safe travels."

I hung up the phone, filled with uneasiness about making the house uninhabitable. Everything that seemed clear was now murky. I groaned. Some days I really hated having a conscience.

Chapter 29

Tuesday, February 22, 1994

It was late morning when I arrived at Allen's house with Charlie in the car. Allen's vintage convertible, newly licensed, sat in the driveway, and Paul's truck was parked in front of the garage. Allen came out of the house. "Paul is driving me in the convertible," he said. "I'm fine driving my truck around town, but my eyesight isn't what it used to be. So, you'll ride back from Ogdensburg in style, though sadly it's not top-down weather."

I swallowed. This man, who saw so many ways to help, who understood so much, couldn't see well at all. The three of us could have ridden in his truck, but he had gone the extra mile so I would be comfortable. "That will be great. I'll look forward to it."

On the drive to Ogdensburg, dark clouds hung over the St. Lawrence River. But they did nothing to dampen Charlie's elation.

"I can't believe I'll live in a place with a view of the river," he said.

"I thought your room was at the back."

"It is, but from the living room and dining room, I'll be able to watch the weather in the winter and the boats in summer."

"And you'll be able to visit Charlene."

"That means a lot. Now that you're a parent, you know that you never stop worrying about your child. I'm assured she's well taken care of, but it will be nice to spend more time with her."

At the assisted-living facility, Mrs. Warren was waiting for us. She took Charlie into the common room and began introducing him to the other residents. Allen and Paul brought his stuff to his new room, where I unpacked it.

When we were done, we found him in the sitting room chatting with one of the residents.

"Charlie, we're done here."

I gave my uncle a quick hug. "I'm heading home tomorrow, but I'll be in touch. You have a phone in your room, and I've taken down the number. And here are your car keys. I've parked right beneath your window."

"There's one more thing I'd like you to do for me before you leave." Charlie smiled. "In that box with the photographs, there's a New York State Police decal. I've noticed that all the walkers here look alike and that everyone has something on theirs to distinguish it from the others."

"Sure. I'll be back in a minute." I went to my uncle's room, returned with the sticker, and helped him attach it to his walker.

"Thanks, Phyl."

I was delighted to see the twinkle in his eyes.

"I've decided that when I sit in the hallway, I can catch speeders."

I laughed at the image of residents speeding up the hall with their walkers. Charlie would enjoy his time at the assisted-living facility.

"I've been thinking about the car," he said. "Thinking perhaps I should give to Miriam's daughter Jill in Oneida. She's one of the good members of the family. She's always been kind to me."

Allen looked at me and rolled his eyes. "Where was she when you needed her?"

I shared his dismay. Charlie might feel guilty about the appliances too, or perhaps just wanted it known that all of Miriam's family weren't like Wally and Verna.

"It's a nice little car," I said calmly. "Why don't you wait and see if you'll be able to drive again? If not, you can sell it. You may need whatever money it brings."

"I've arranged for the Watertown paper to be delivered to you each morning," Allen chimed in. "And if you want any furniture from your storage area, just say the word. I'll bring it to you."

"You better get on the road before it storms," Charlie said.

"Call me if you need me," I said with a last hug. It wasn't easy leaving Charlie, but I sensed he was eager to begin his new life. And he was right. The clouds were massing.

Allen and I talked little in his convertible as Paul drove to Agnes's house. I was drained, and Allen seemed to share my tiredness.

"I'll take you to the airport tomorrow," he said.

"I'd appreciate it."

Allen removed the 1754 coin from his pocket. "It's shiny now. I wire brushed it."

I inspected it. The wire bushing had totally obliterated the date on the coin. His desire to clean it had made the coin worthless to anyone but me. It was so like this very special man to want the coin to be in order for me.

I closed my fist around it. "I'll treasure it, Allen. Now, there's one other thing. Could we go by the storage area tomorrow? Charlie wanted me to take the family silver home. I'd completely forgotten about it."

"Sure thing," he said.

In Carthage, Agnes must have been watching for us, because she came out on the porch.

"Don't let Allen leave just yet. I have something for him."

He got out of the convertible. Agnes emerged from the house with her hands full. "I've used your apples to make you a pie."

Allen smiled and took it. "It's been a long while since I've had a homemade apple pie. Thank you."

Agnes's pie reminded me of the network of mutual help that Allen had in place. I gave her a thumbs up.

Allen carefully placed the pie on the floorboard of the car. "Phyllis, I'll see you tomorrow morning at about nine."

Heavy snow began to fall like a window shade suddenly being pulled down. "Drive safely, I said with a farewell wave.

While we were eating dinner, I heard pellets of ice pummeling the roof and rattling the window frame. I gave an exaggerated groan, and then shook my head.

Chapter 30

Wednesday, February 23, 1994

I awoke the next morning to the welcome sound of steady rain. It had warmed during the night, and the snow turned to rain. I dressed, had breakfast with Agnes, and packed everything except Charlie's poster-sized, framed picture.

"I'm not sure I can get this home," I said when I brought it and my suitcase downstairs.

"I've been thinking about that," Agnes said. "We'll wrap it in brown paper."

Agnes found scissors and cut up several grocery bags with practiced skill. In minutes, she covered the picture and taped the paper in place. "And I've got just the thing to help you carry it. I saved a pair of pantyhose that you threw away. They'll be like a gigantic rubber band."

She located the washed pantyhose. She cut it up and further secured the paper around the picture.

"There."

I couldn't help but smile at her resourcefulness – and at the thought of walking through the Pittsburg airport with a package wrapped in pantyhose.

"I've prepared a little lunch for you to take with you." From nowhere, Agnes produced a shoebox.

I peeked inside and saw sandwiches and freshly baked cookies.

"You're a dear. I don't know how I would have managed in the last weeks without you." I gave her a big hug.

At that moment, Allen arrived at the door and took my bag.

"Your pie was delicious," he said to Agnes. "I'll give you a call when we get *our girl* on the plane."

Agnes waved us off. A half-hour later, we pulled up in front of the storage area.

"I know right where the silver is," Allen said. "I put it in one of the dressers. Stay in the car out of the rain. I'll bring it to you."

Minutes later, he deposited the silver on my lap. While he locked up, I opened the box, then rolled down the window

"Wait a minute, Allen. I'm not taking this with me."

"What's the matter?"

I laughed grimly. "It's not the family sterling with its "H" on every piece. It's silverplate. Wally substituted this junk cutlery for the family heirloom." In one fell swoop, the guilty feelings I had about the appliances vanished.

"Do you want me to confront him about it?"

"No. I'm just happy to be done with my uncle's second family. Let Wally think he's put something over on me."

"I'm glad Charlie is out of town. Otherwise, Miriam's family still might be leaching off him."

He returned it to the dresser and we headed to the airport at Dexter. The same little, puddle-jumper plane was on the tarmac.

"I've got something for your husband," Allen said as passengers began to board. "New York State cheese, cheese curd, and Croghan baloney." He handed me a package.

"I could not have liberated my uncle, his car, and furniture from that bunch without your sage advice, strong arm, constant support, and local contacts."

"After decades, Hall and Hodge joined forces again. I don't think *those people* knew what they were in for."

"What will you do now that you have your life back?"

"I'll be lonely," he said.

I gave him a heartfelt goodbye hug, assembled my various packages, and boarded the plane. As I settled into my seat for the take-off, I found it hard to get the silver out of my mind. Throughout the whole ordeal, the stakes for Charlie had been huge. His life, for one thing. His dignity for another. No one liked to be taken advantage of.

In the urgency of the last days, I regretted that I hadn't more forcefully pursued the possibility that Wally or Verna had done something to hasten Charlie's death. Whenever I mentioned either of them to my uncle, it was clear that he had no use for them and didn't want to talk about his time with them. When I brought up the possibility of poisoning to a doctor, he had been dismissive, blaming Charlie's problems on his advanced age. Stonewalled by Charlie and the doctor, I didn't probe any further.

I waved to Allen from the small, rain-streaked window. It had taken Odysseus twenty years to return home, and my odyssey had only taken 20 days. And although I was weary and ready to return to my family, I had the satisfaction of realizing that what I had done would have made my father, who never suffered fools gladly, proud.

They tell me I am going to die.
My cup is full. Let it spill.
　　　　My Cup *by Robert Friend*

Epilogue

September 30, 1996

I sat in my office looking out at leaves swirling in the wind. Charlie's funeral had been two weeks ago. Now both he and Allen have gone to the great hereafter. When I left Watertown that February, I wasn't through with them. I didn't join a church after my experience with Gideon and Charlie's sudden turnaround. But I never forgot what had happened, and believe now, as then, that Charlie and I had a profound spiritual experience, and that the ancient wisdom found in the book of Job helped us both. Instead of going to church every Sunday morning, I called Allen and Charlie.

Two months after Charlie went to live in Ogdensburg, Allen asked his permission to move his possessions from the storage area to the farm in Croghan. Charlie was relieved to no

211

longer have to pay a monthly storage fee. No doubt the real purpose of our visit to the farm was to assure me of its suitability to store my uncle's things. Allen, as throughout the whole ordeal, had been one step ahead of me.

Charlie did drive his car again. Charlene's United Helpers nursing facility was three miles away for his new residence. He triumphantly drove to see her every third day. And I was delighted that, for a few moments, however fleeting, Charlie was again master of his fate.

A year later, I had another emergency trip to Northern New York when Charlie fell and broke his neck. I visited him in the Syracuse hospital where he was encased in one of those terrible birdcages that people wear after this kind of accident. He was miserable, but interestingly, he never said he wanted to die.

After his broken neck, Charlie moved to a nursing home in the United Helpers network. He sold his car to one of the United Helpers' employees, bonded with the staff, and remained in sound mind. He was able to visit Charlene and never had stomach problems again, despite his fondness for oranges and peppermint candies. I sent him some often, even though Internet research revealed that they were on the list of the worst foods for people who have a hiatal hernia. His filled candy dish became a favorite destination for nurses and aides.

On the occasions that I visited Allen, he never let me photograph him. In vain, I searched through Dad's Trooper photos for a picture of him. Nonetheless, I sent him pictures of me. He told me he had leukemia and asked me not to let my uncle know. It was hard, but I honored his wishes.

Toward the end of his life, his daughter, Susanne, wisely arranged for a cook to come to his house, and where he hadn't eaten much for years, in his last days, he enjoyed home cooking. When people are dying, things like good food make a huge difference. With chemotherapy, radiation, and hospitalizations, sometimes the simple things, the ordinary blessings, get overlooked. I liked to think my weekly calls were among Allen's blessings.

When I learned from his daughter that he was near the end of life, I drove the 600 miles to Watertown in the bleak December of 1995 to see him one last time. He was confined to a wheelchair, and despite his illness, he retained his equanimity, good cheer, and involvement in life. We talked for two hours. He told me about a younger brother who died after being hit by a streetcar and about the flu epidemic of 1918. It occurred to me that I could live a long time and never again hear first-hand about a person being killed by a streetcar or about the flu epidemic. That upbeat visit was Allen's final gift to me.

After he died, Susanne told me they had buried my pictures with him. His properties were auctioned off and along with them, Charlie's possessions at the Croghan house. It seemed proper. Not that a collection of old furniture could repay Allen for all he had done. Hopefully though, if anything was realized from their sale, it went to support his wife, who outlived him.

One night the following July, I received a call that my uncle had been taken to the hospital with congestive heart failure. They didn't keep him, and when I spoke with him the next morning, he told me, "I love you." I guessed the end was near since he'd never told me that before.

Later that summer, Charlie was running through all of his savings. His expenses during the last year had been $36,000 and his State Police Retirement wasn't enough to be of much help. I visited him and went through the whole process of applying for Medicaid.

Charlie had always been able to pay his own way. For him, receiving Medicaid was equivalent to being on welfare.

Then, in a surprising and generous move, the New York State Legislature upped the retirement benefits for a handful of old State Troopers who had served long years and had small yearly pensions. So once again, Charlie's dignity was restored. He was jubilant that he was able to pay his own way, at least for a while. He was also notified that he was the oldest living Trooper in the state.

In early September, I had talked with my uncle the Sunday before he died. He was full of enthusiasm. He had watched the best college football game he'd ever seen the day before. Later that week, he was taken to the hospital again with congestive heart failure. The doctor asked him if he wanted extraordinary measures to prolong his life, and he said "no." I would never know whether, in the end, Charlie had believed, as Gideon had told him, that his life belonged to God, or if he just wanted to die with dignity. Possibly, he just may have wanted to leave the earth before his money ran out. Whatever had happened, his decision came not from a place of defeat, but rather from a place of strength. I felt proud of him. He had accepted the inevitable with grace and dignity, not in the depth of despair with vultures circling.

The September sun shone brightly for Charlie's memorial service at Brookside Cemetery, a lovely place with rolling hills and a duck pond. His ashes were interred next to his first wife. The State Troopers turned out in numbers for a quasi-military service. Agnes was there, as was Ross, along with a few of Charlie's old neighbors and some distant cousins. Allen's daughter, Elizabeth from Connecticut, who happened to be in town visiting her mother, extended her stay to attend the funeral. Surprisingly, several of Miriam's family attended, including Jill. I thought their presence may have signaled their approval of how I had rescued my uncle, but knew that Allen would have said they had *some nerve* showing up.

My son, Alex, had taken photographs of the ceremony. I spread them out on my desk and studied them. I'd not seen Wally at the funeral. But I spied him in the photos, lurking about the edges of the crowd. He hadn't spoken with me. Did he think I'd say something about the silver? Wally's shadowing of the service seemed to fit perfectly with what I knew of him. Verna and her branch of the family didn't show. Why should they? They had nothing to gain.

If this were a mystery novel, I would have found proof that Verna or Wally had interfered with Charlie's medicines or fed him something lethal. But real life is a lot more complicated than fiction. I never would know, and wish I could convince myself that it was all in my imagination. Yet people had done worse for less than an old house and a few antiques. Anyway, it didn't really matter what they had done, or not. Their very presence had been killing him.

I put the photos away, stood, and looked out at my yard. One time, when I had visited Charlie in the nursing home, he had insisted — even though it was raining — that I pick up crabapples from a tree in the courtyard. He wanted me to plant them and eventually enjoy their luxurious spring flowering, as he had in his days in the nursing home.

My eyes sought out the crabapple sapling, still alive, but a long way from blooming. A skeptic would say that all my efforts were for naught, that it was all the same in the end. But I knew that wasn't true. The Roman philosopher Seneca wrote what would be a good motto for hospice: "As is a tale, so is life: not how long it is, but how good it is, is what matters."

This has been Charlie's story, but it was also my story. Dealing with his situation, I reinforced what I had learned as a hospice volunteer. Every life, even one as seemingly uneventful as my mild-mannered uncle's, was special, and all one could do at the end was to help make the last days as rich and full as possible.

As importantly, I was able to put behind me the mistaken belief that I'd never lived up to my father's expectations and never gained his approval. I had learned that I was very much like him. I guessed he'd always known that, even if he wasn't able to articulate it, but it was something I had to learn.

Several months after Allen died, I received a package in the mail from his daughter, Elizabeth. She sent me her father's refrigerator magnet of Lake Bonaparte. Now I have two identical magnets, a shiny coin, a framed photo of Charlie as a young Trooper astride his horse, and the promise of spring blossoms. Sometimes my riches astound me.

Acknowledgements

Over the years I have been working on this book, I had help and encouragement from many people. The author of ROSSIO SQUARE No. 59, Jeannine Johnson Mia, busy overseeing the publication of her second novel, honored me by over 2000 questions, suggestions, and feedback. It is a great compliment for someone to take your work seriously. Thank you, Jeannine!

Other writers, Russ and Peg Hall, Thayer Cory-Weet, and Suzi Stembridge kindly read the book in various forms and offered suggestions, comments, and concerns. Check out their books on Amazon. Russ and Peg write about the Camino de Santiago, Russ about cheese and Star Lake in the Adirondacks, Thayer is thoughtful poet, and Suzi writes novels and memoirs set in Greece.

100 Covers provided the gorgeous cover while Rebecca at Indiemobi the expert formatting.

Thanks to my husband, Otis, who continues to encourage my writing.

About the Author

This is my tenth, published book and writing doesn't get any easier.

I first wrote this book as narrative nonfiction, distancing myself from the story. At that time, I thought it was my uncle's story. I gradually learned it was my story, too. So, I rewrote it as a memoir, hoping that would enhance the emotional truth of the events.

I am always happy to hear from readers. Contact me at: Phytllis.haislip@gmail.com

Made in the USA
Middletown, DE
24 December 2022